WOMAN TO WOMAN

WOMAN

W♀MAN

THE TRUTH ABOUT
OUR INTIMATE RELATIONSHIPS:

How We Love, Hurt And Triumph

DANIELA GRANZOTTO, Psy.D

NEW YORK

WOMAN TO WOMAN

THE TRUTH ABOUT OUR INTIMATE RELATIONSHIPS:
How We Love, Hurt And Triumph

by DANIELA GRANZOTTO, Psy.D

ISBN 978-1-61448-175-1 Paperback
Library of Congress Control Number: 2011943663

Published by:
MORGAN JAMES PUBLISHING
The Entrepreneurial Publisher
5 Penn Plaza, 23rd Floor
New York City, New York 10001
(212) 655-5470 Office
(516) 908-4496 Fax
www.MorganJamesPublishing.com

Cover Design by:
Rachel Lopez
www.r2cdesign.com

Interior Design by:
Bonnie Bushman
bonnie_bushman@optimum.net

To my parents, Clovis and Marilene, with love.

Acknowledgements

I would like to express my deepest gratitude to all of the women who shared their personal stories. Their willingness and openness to talk about their romantic experiences greatly enriched this book. To preserve their anonymity, I have altered their names and certain identifying details.

Special thanks to literary agent Kristina Holmes for believing in my work and guiding me in the right direction.

I am grateful to my children, Myla and Taj, for filling my heart with immense love. And to my husband, Andrew, who always found time to read my work and polish it along the way.

CONTENTS

Introduction

We all have, in our core, a longing for love. When we develop a deep romantic connection, we experience a sense of comfort and belonging.

While most of us will bond with a partner at some point in our lives, not all of us will experience true love. A lasting and gratifying union is only possible when critical elements of a healthy relationship are present. Otherwise, deep disappointment is inevitable.

Dissatisfaction with romantic love is rather common among women. When they come to see me for therapy, some are discontent with their unhealthy relationships, while others are frustrated for not being able to find that special someone. Many claim to have lost a feeling of closeness with their significant other and are unsure of how to reconnect.

My inspiration in writing this book came from working with these women and understanding that while they are unique individuals, when it comes to love, they are not so different. All women experience joy, frustration and disappointment in their romantic lives. They share a strong desire to find love, but often times are unable to fulfill this most important area of their lives.

This book addresses major challenges women face in their relationships, such as the end of a marriage, infidelity and marital conflict. It examines the root causes of their difficulties and provides an intimate discussion on the key elements of a rewarding relationship. Fear of intimacy and commitment, ineffective communication, and inadequate self-esteem, are some of the areas that are examined in detail.

When I contemplated writing this book, I felt strongly about having women of different ages and marital status share about romantic love. My intention was to provide the reader an opportunity to relate to other women's experiences. In the end, the interviews shaped the content and chapters of the book.

Through the testimonials you will learn what makes a woman's marriage a success, while others experience major disappointment. You will hear from women who are in unhealthy relationships and those who, despite major hurt, were able to rebuild their lives.

As you read their personal accounts, you may find that their stories resemble your own. While each woman's love life has its own twists and turns, we all love, struggle and hurt in similar ways.

Dr. Daniela Granzotto

Married and Lonely

When a Relationship Lacks Emotional Intimacy

Men and woman share a longing for love, but differ in how they experience intimate relationships. Women look forward to the feeling of closeness with a partner—talking, exchanging affection, and spending time together is of utmost importance.

Women tend to place a great value on their relationships, which can be explained by the childhood role models and early messages they internalize while growing up. As girls, they learn the importance of being nurturing and attuned to other people's feelings.

Men, on the other hand, are raised to value independence and self-reliance. They learn to bond through shared activities as opposed to talking and expressing feelings. Career and achievement are important to them.

Compared to women, men are not as in tune with their feelings and those of others. They also tend to have difficulty understanding emotions that are not openly verbalized. When it comes to intimate relationships, the level of closeness they expect is often not on par with that of women.

That is not to say that a man is any less capable of developing an emotional bond with the person he loves. Just like well adjusted women, emotionally healthy men welcome intimacy. They allow themselves to become close to their partners without fearing the loss of their own identity. Their relationships contain trust, respect, affection and open communication, which is what emotional intimacy is all about.

While emotional intimacy is the foundation of every lasting and satisfying union, it is certainly lacking in a great number of relationships. Why is this so?

Our early childhood experiences have a significant impact on our love lives. In other words, the view we internalized of ourselves and the emotional difficulties we experienced shape who we are and how we behave in our relationships.

As children, we turn to our caregivers for food, comfort, and love. If they are able to meet our needs, we develop a sense of trust and security. We feel their love for us and this in turn makes us feel worthy and secure in our lovability.

Being raised in such a warm environment has a positive influence on the partners we become involved with and how we relate to them. We are likely to attract and be attracted to individuals capable of being emotionally intimate. We allow ourselves to trust and get close to our partners. When conflict arises, we are likely to solve it effectively through respect and compromise. As a result, we tend to be satisfied with our intimate relationships.

Not all of us, however, had the best upbringing. Some of us had parents who were rejecting or inconsistent in their ability to make us feel safe, unconditionally loved, and cared for. These early experiences affect our ability to trust and feel worthy of love.

Our low sense of self-worth increases our fear of rejection and abandonment and compels us to stay in an unhappy and unhealthy relationship longer than we desire.

Mary, 55, shares her experience of being in an unfulfilling marriage. Immersed within her testimonial are the words of a woman who holds a poor view of herself:

> I don't love Fred, I don't think I ever did. He's not my companion or the man I wanted for myself. I wish he was my friend and respected me. We have nothing in common. We have a lot of conflict in our marriage and I resent him very much. But what can I do at this point in my life? It's not good being with him, but it would be worse without him. I don't want to start all over again with someone else. I'm no longer young and pretty. I don't have anything to offer.

People's fears and insecurities originated from childhood can also interfere with their ability to emotionally attach to a partner and fully commit to the relationship.

Linda, 42, is married to an emotionally distant partner:

> My husband comes home and goes straight to the TV, he doesn't even talk with us. He does the same thing when we go out to eat. He sits at the table and grabs his newspaper, he ignores us. He never has time for his family. His life is all about work. I feel angry. It's not fair, it's not right what he's doing.

Individuals who experience strong feelings of inferiority and inadequacy may also have a need to control their partners. Their domination can take the form of emotional, physical, or sexual abuse.

Claire, 32, is married to an abusive partner:

> My husband is controlling and abusive. He makes negative comments and criticizes me about every little thing I do. He also makes hurtful jokes with the intention of humiliating me. I feel like I'm being treated like a child and I don't like it all. I experience a lot of anger and resentment toward him. I'm very unhappy in my marriage.

Since healthy intimacy constitutes the core of a gratifying relationship, there are ways for you and your partner to nourish a strong foundation. The first step is to reflect on what has been preventing both of you from experiencing an emotional connection with one another.

As mentioned before, our early experiences with our caregivers have a great deal of influence on our intimate relationships. If we internalize a view of ourselves as being unworthy, defective, and unlovable, we are going to find it extremely difficult to trust a partner and become emotionally close to him. We will be inclined to perceive his behavior as insincere, rejecting, and uncaring. Our low self-esteem also increases our chances to get involved with unhealthy partners.

Therefore, when building intimacy in your relationship, you need to ask yourself the following questions: What are the faulty assumptions that interfere with my ability to develop intimacy? Is it the belief that I am not good enough to be loved? Is it the fear of being rejected and having to deal with immense pain and hurt? Or is it the dread of being controlled and losing myself?

We all feel the need to develop a meaningful relationship with another human being to experience a sense of connection and belonging. If we fail, we are likely to feel lonely.

Being lonely, however, is not the same as being alone. While alone, we have the opportunity to reflect on how we feel and think about ourselves, our relationships, and our lives in general. Being alone can be a meaningful and enriching experience.

Loneliness, on the other hand, is an emotional state that involves feelings of isolation, emptiness, and alienation. We feel disconnected from others. When we feel lonely, we may experience sadness, depression, anxiety, and low self-esteem. These feelings can lead to self-destructive behaviors, like the excessive use of alcohol, food, or drugs.

Many women experience loneliness, including those who are married. We may feel lonely when our spouses are often away on business trips, work late hours, or pursue their own interests. The lack of time together makes it difficult for us to develop a strong bond with our loved one.

We may also feel lonely if our partner is physically present yet emotionally distant. When we fail in our attempts to be noticed and heard, we are likely to experience strong feelings of rejection, emptiness, and sadness. This is the case with Betsy, 48, married for twenty-three years:

> My husband and I haven't had a nice conversation
> in a long time. He can sit right next to me for hours
> without saying a word. When we talk, it's always

about the kids, bills to be paid, and other insignificant things. I don't feel important to him. I feel lonely. I wish he would pay attention to me like he used to when we were dating. He made me feel special. Now he doesn't even notice me anymore. I've tried to talk to him about how I feel, but he shuts me out. I feel unhappy in my marriage.

Carol, 36, shares her frustration of being unable to connect with her spouse:

I've been married for twelve years. This is what a typical day with my husband is like for the past several years:

My husband gets home around 6:00pm. He says hi to me and the kids and goes to change. Then he sits at the table to have dinner. Usually he asks, "What's for dinner today?" I hate that question. Sometimes I say something like dead roach soup and gecko sandwiches. He laughs. I ask myself, what the hell is he laughing at? Does he think I'm trying to be funny?

At the table he asks me about my day. I know all he wants to hear is that my day was good. If I extend myself, he seems to get annoyed and tells me to get to the point. He frequently interrupts me to say something to the kids and doesn't show any interest in having me continue what I was saying. This is upsetting. He makes me feel that what I have to say isn't important.

After dinner the kids go to sleep and we sit on the couch. First thing he does is turn on the TV. It's like he has a meeting with the TV every day. He doesn't ask me what I want to watch. He goes ahead and turns to sports, which I have no interest in. What I hate even more is when he's watching TV and his attention isn't on me. I don't think it's asking too much of him to just look at me when I'm talking. If I ask him a question, I have to repeat it because at first it doesn't register in his brain. What is it that men can only focus on one thing at a time? The other day I asked if he could chew gum and walk at the same time and he got upset.

I tried to talk to him about how I feel. He told me "Okay, I'll turn off the TV." He then turned to me and said, "So what do you want to say?" He got it all wrong. By telling him how I felt, I thought he would say "Okay, honey, I understand how you feel and I'll do things differently to make you happy." However, it didn't work that way. So things continued the way they were. While he's watching TV, I wait for the commercials to talk to him. Lately, however, he's been recording his TV shows and he can skip through the commercials. So all I can do is try to remember everything I want to tell him and wait until after his show ends.

By the time he finishes watching TV it's time to go to bed. In bed I have about two minutes of his attention if I'm lucky. Usually it takes him about five seconds to fall asleep. He tries hard to keep his eyes open for about two minutes so I can talk. His brain, however, is already sleeping and it's just his eyes that are open. I used to think that he was listening because he was so quiet. But I realized that he's just going in and out of sleep. Once I stop talking, the room gets quiet for a few moments. He then kisses me goodnight and tells me he loves me. The only time he talks to me for as long as I want is when he wants to have sex. He knows he needs to talk to me first to get what he wants.

I do love my husband and I know he loves me, but I wish he would sit down with me for a few moments every day without turning on the TV or interrupting me. I don't mind the routine of my marriage—I was expecting that before I made the decision to get married. What I wasn't expecting was the fact that I wouldn't be able to count on my husband as my companion and best friend.

A couple's success in connecting with each other depends on both people's willingness to reach out to one another.

As mentioned before, some people have difficulty allowing themselves to get close to the person they love. They may fear being smothered and controlled or being rejected and abandoned.

People who experience a strong fear of rejection tend to believe they are not good enough to be loved. While they think they are trying everything possible to bond with their partners, they may engage in behavior that drives their significant others away. They do this to protect themselves from what they see as inevitable rejection. This self-protective behavior, however, can lead to loneliness.

It is in our early years that we first experience loneliness. It happens when we feel neglected and rejected by those we love most. The inability to reach out to important people in our lives perpetuates feelings of disconnection and isolation.

Trust is destroyed and, to protect ourselves from further pain, we retreat.

As the years pass and we reach adulthood, our appearance changes, but we still feel the same inside, afraid to get close to the person we love for fear of being rejected and abandoned.

Our past emotional wounds, therefore, can interfere with our ability to develop meaningful relationships and thus contributes to our feelings of isolation. For these reason we need to heal. The healing process begins with revisiting our past and allowing ourselves to get in touch with painful experiences and feelings. We work on the present by identifying dysfunctional and inaccurate thoughts, beliefs, and behaviors that feed our feelings of fear, anger, and shame. We replace them with more realistic and empowering statements and behaviors.

When healing begins to take place, we witness ourselves growing into a more self-confident and well- balanced person who feels empowered to make positive changes. While our wounds may never be completely healed, they can be repaired to the point that our negative emotions no longer force decisions upon us.

For a long time, Barbara, a 39-year-old psychologist, carried unresolved emotional wounds from her childhood. In her journey toward healing, she was able to face her fears and forgive an important person in her life. She learned not to feel like a powerless victim of the past, but rather a truly proud survivor:

> Most of the memories I have about my childhood are sad. When I go back and visit my past, I remember seeing a child who perceived the world as being full of strangers. I felt insecure, inadequate, and worthless.

My father was affectionate toward me, but had difficulty controlling his anger. He never laid a hand on me, but I was afraid of him. When he yelled, he did so loudly. My mother was less affectionate, but showed more empathy. However, her mood swings were difficult to live with. I never knew when she was going to wake up on the wrong side of the bed. When she did, she was irritable and impatient. This created a lot of anxiety in me.

My parents showed their love mostly through their concern about my health. My mother was critical of me, and I felt I didn't live up to her expectations.

I felt I was a sick and defective child. How could I feel good about myself if I wasn't good enough for my parents? I wanted them to be proud of me, but I felt that I had failed. For many years in my life, I suffered the agony of never being perfect in the eyes of my mother and, worst of all, in my own eyes.

Because of my feelings of inferiority and lack of self-confidence I struggled in all areas of my life for a long time. I felt devastated when I didn't get a good grade. I felt ugly and not good enough to believe that boys were interested in me. I had difficulty seeing that I had friends who cared about me. Because of my feelings of inadequacy, I created a wall around me.

When I became involved in romantic relationships, I expected my significant other to be the perfect partner. I tried, in vain, to change them to fit my ideal version of a man. I had a strong fear of being rejected. Being close to someone was frightening to me. When I started getting involved with a nice guy I would end the relationship because I believed that he would eventually get tired of me and leave. The more insecure and afraid I was, the lonelier I felt.

It wasn't until I moved out of my parents' house and reexamined my past that I began to change the way I felt about myself. I've been able to slowly build up my self-esteem. I've accomplished goals that I once thought were impossible. I married a great man, and I feel secure about his love for me.

Over the years I've been able to look at my past and the current relationship with my parents from another perspective. I no longer see my mother with the eyes of a child. She no longer has the power she once had over me. Likewise, I learned not to fear my dad, but instead understand that behind his outbursts there's a person who never learned how to deal with fear, anxiety, and frustration.

A few years ago my mother sat down with me and talked about her childhood, her marriage, and her unfulfilled dreams. She shared her resentment of not being able to change her past and her feelings of hopelessness about the future. I was profoundly touched by the deepness of her wounds.

For many years I blamed my parents for not giving me the childhood that I felt I deserved. Fortunately, I've been able to let go of the anger and resentment. I understand that, like me, my parents were once children who also had less then perfect parents.

Unlike me, my mother hasn't been able to heal and create a new life for herself. She'll probably die believing that life is not worth living. I wish she could have healed her wounds just enough to allow her to stop bleeding.

As for me, I'm glad that I no longer feel victimized by my past. On the bright side, if I had a different past, I wouldn't be exactly where I am now, which is where I want to be.

For Barbara and many of us, our childhood lacks the warm memories we need to grow into a person with solid self-esteem. Nevertheless, we always have the option of changing the way we feel about ourselves.

When we learn our own worth, a new world unfolds. We feel empowered to pursue meaningful things and to experience love in a mature and healthy manner. Moments of fear, insecurity, and loneliness should not be seen as a reflection of our unlovability or worthlessness, but rather as a reminder that it doesn't have to be this way.

"I felt like a sex object"

When Boundaries Are Violated

Many women see their marriages change from an experience of personal fulfillment to a source of extreme frustration and discontent. But are we all doomed to endure painful disappointment in our marriages?

It takes two people for a relationship to work, and both need to have a good sense of self-worth. When we see ourselves in a positive light, we can give and receive love. We are able to set boundaries and show similar respect to our partner without fear of rejection and abandonment. Solid self-esteem also helps us deal with relationship conflicts and life difficulties.

Having a good sense of self-worth, however, does not imply that we will never question how we feel about ourselves. We all have our moments of insecurity and self- doubt. For those of us who have poor self-esteem, these moments can happen quite often. This is especially true if we are in an intimate relationship with a partner who is neglectful and treats us with little respect.

His hurtful and uncaring behavior can exacerbate our feelings of inadequacy while decreasing our marital satisfaction.

Dissatisfaction with our relationship can have a negative impact on many areas of our lives: work, family and motherhood. It is hard for those of us who are mothers to be the best caretaker if our romantic life is not going well. How can we nurture our children if we are not nurtured by our mate? How can we look at ourselves and feel special if our partner keeps saying otherwise through his actions or behavior? An unhealthy relationship can lead us to experience a range of feelings including anger, hurt, and sadness.

It is in our state of deep sadness that we are likely to find ourselves feeling hopeless and helpless. We feel discouraged, confused, and fearful. However, regardless of how intense these feelings are, they should not be seen as a sign of weakness, but rather an indication that something is not working in our lives and ought to be changed. Saying "enough" to anything or anyone that causes us deep pain and sadness can be a major step in the right direction, bringing us closer to what is truly meaningful.

Sarah, a 37-year-old mother of three, shares about her unhealthy marriage and how she stood up for herself:

> The beginning of my marriage was great. Steven and I started having babies right away, and I was happy because I wanted to have children. We did a lot of moving because of his job. I supported him and I followed him. I took care of the kids and worked full-time.
>
> Back then our relationship was okay. Steven was a good husband. At times, however, he was

too controlling and stressed about money. He also complained a lot about our sex life. It's always been his biggest complaint.

Steven never felt he had enough sex. Even if I gave him a lot, he still complained. He was never satisfied. This was discouraging because no matter how hard I tried, it was never enough. At a certain point I felt like not trying anymore because he was going to complain anyway. He made me feel like shit.

I've always felt like a sex object to my husband. He said that he felt I never loved him, which is not true. However, I may have put a wall around my heart just like I did with everything else, because I didn't feel I was being treated with respect. I felt I was being treated like a child.

In my relationship with Steven, nothing was private, and that upset me. I think a married couple should have intimacy only in the bedroom. They should treat each other with respect in front of the children; you don't go and grab and make comments in front of the kids.

Steven, however, did that. I felt he was so denigrating to me. Like in the morning when we were fixing breakfast for the kids, he would come over and grab me. To me it was inappropriate, and I guess he felt rejected. He would say something mean like "You better put out soon or I'll find someone else." This happened a lot in the last two or three years of our marriage.

While feeling like a second class citizen, I was happy in my marriage; I was content. I tolerated it because that's what I thought women do. They just kind of go along with it. I was going to school. I was trying to do things that were making me happy because I learned from therapy you can't depend on other people for your happiness. But Steven wanted me to be his trophy, the young pretty girl, and this was difficult for me to accept. He wanted me to go to parties with him and show me off, like on his fiftieth birthday.

Right before his party Steven took me out shopping. He dressed me up in the clothes he wanted me to wear. I looked like a twelve-year-old slut. He took me out to dinner and tried to get me drunk. We went dancing, and he wanted me to dance with other guys, and I did. I didn't want to be treated that way, but I went along because it was his fiftieth.

I got totally drunk, then he wanted to go to a strip bar and I refused. I said, "I'm done; I can't even see straight." He was pissed and left me inside the car in the parking lot where I fell asleep. Two hours later I woke up and I had no idea where he was. I called him on his cell phone and he was so furious I didn't do what he planned. He called me a fucking bitch. I left him and found a ride home.

I've never had good boundaries with my husband. It was so hard to set boundaries without making myself look mean. I always felt guilty. If I had better boundaries, I would probably never have married Steven.

I wish I could have felt good enough about myself not to be treated with disrespect, like a sexual object.

However, I was so afraid of not being loved, of not having anybody. I wanted to please Steven all the time, but I was failing. This made me feel depressed to the point that I couldn't take it anymore.

Steven wanted me to do whatever he wanted and, if I didn't, he wasn't happy. After therapy, I realized that it wasn't okay for me anymore. I started fighting back and no longer let him control me. I started putting up boundaries and respecting myself. Steven, on the other hand, was getting more and more unhappy.

None of us should be satisfied with a relationship in which we feel neglected and mistreated. Such a relationship lacks trust and respect, which is at the core of a healthy and satisfying union.

When we feel respected and reassured of our desirability and lovability, we allow ourselves to get emotionally and physically close to our significant other. We trust our partner and are not afraid of exposing ourselves.

Our ability to trust and attract partners who are trustworthy is related to our sense of self-worth. If we experience strong feelings of inadequacy and worthlessness we are likely to attract partners who are not sincere, honest or respectful. We may question their love for us and have difficulty setting boundaries.

A relationship that lacks healthy boundaries is doomed to fail. What about your boundaries, have you defined them with your partner?

All of us need to make clear what our boundaries are as well as communicate and enforce them. Likewise, we need to know our partner's boundaries and respect them as well.

Kelly, 34, made her boundaries clear to her spouse:

> In the beginning of my relationship with Tom, I told him that I wouldn't tolerate any form of abuse. I can't see myself staying in a relationship with someone who puts me down and makes me feel bad about myself. If there's no respect, there's no love. I also believe in fidelity, and I made it clear to my husband that there wouldn't be a second chance if he was unfaithful to me.

The purpose of setting boundaries with our spouse is to protect ourselves from being disrespected, abused or controlled. When we set boundaries, we are communicating through our words and actions how we expect to be treated and what behaviors are unacceptable.

Some people may resist their spouse's attempts to set boundaries. This is likely the case when a person has a strong need to be in control.

If you are in a relationship with someone who is unwilling to accept your boundaries, perhaps you should end it. While it can be a very difficult thing to do, it is best to grieve the loss of an unhealthy relationship than to remain with a partner who gives you no chance of experiencing a healthy, intimate bond.

Janice, 32, decided to separate from her husband when his judgmental and rejecting behavior toward her became unbearable. When they reunited, their relationship no longer resembled the one they once had:

> I always dreamed about getting married and having kids. I wanted to have my own family. I dropped out

of school during my second year of college to get married. I married a wonderful man who was in love with me. Paul was smart, caring, and loving. We were soul mates. The first five years of our marriage were wonderful. During that time we had our first child and we were happy.

As time passed, however, things gradually started to change. We became increasingly irritable with each other and more demanding. We compromised less and expected more from each other. Paul changed the most. He became more aggressive and less caring and loving. He started seeking me out less and less for sex. I felt he was distancing himself from me.

Paul criticized everything about me: my hair, my clothes, my friends, and my family. He wanted me to be on a diet because he thought I was too fat. He also wanted me to use makeup because he thought I was too pale. He was constantly making comments about my appearance. I started feeling insecure. I realized then how much he had changed since we first met.

As Paul started growing cold and distant, I began to suspect he was having an affair. When I confronted him, he denied it. However, to my surprise, he confessed that he was feeling suffocated, that he had lost his freedom to do whatever he liked. He told me he wanted to hang out with his friends and come home whenever he wanted.

He also said he would like me to take care of myself like I used to. He wanted me to be more sensual and exciting to satisfy his sexual fantasies. I realized that sex was the most important thing in his life. I got upset because I felt like a sex object. I realized that he didn't care about anything I was doing at home—taking care of the house, of our child, and all the other responsibilities he delegated to me. He probably never thought I could feel too tired to have sex.

I was so upset and hurt by everything he said and expected from me that I gained the courage to see a psychologist. Being in therapy helped a lot. I learned that to have a good relationship with my husband I needed to first feel good about myself.

I decided then that I had to give our marriage a break and take care of myself. I moved in with my parents, and for six months I barely saw my husband. In the meantime I built up my self-esteem. I began to find peace within myself. As timed passed, my love for my husband started slowly fading away, and I no longer thought about staying married.

We had been separated for almost a year when, one day, my husband came over to my parents' house and asked me to come back home. He said that he loved me and needed me, and that we should give our marriage another chance. He asked me to think about our son. I thought about it and decided to move back in with him. However, I made it clear that I wasn't the same person I used to be. I had changed a lot during the time we were separated. I set conditions to go back. I told him I wanted to be able to go out with my friends, go back to college, and have time for myself. He agreed.

It's been eight months since we got back together. So far, it's been wonderful. I feel like I've been born again. I'm back in school, and I feel beautiful and attractive. I know what I like and want for myself.

I enjoy seeing the look on my husband's face every day. He just watches me doing everything I like. I no longer give him the right to criticize me or tell me I need to change. He now treats me with respect and appreciation. Our relationship is going well. Let's see what the future holds for us.

Many of us can relate to what Janice experienced during her marriage—feelings of happiness eventually turning into sadness, hurt, and resentment.

Like a number of married women, Janice once experienced a strong bond with her husband. The emotional connection, however, was lost when they were no longer able to show their love for one another. Janice and her husband engaged in behavior that is a sure-fire recipe for an unfulfilling marriage: constant demands, criticism, and not enough understanding, compromise, appreciation, and respect.

Janice had her boundaries violated when her husband created doubts in her mind about her desirability and lovability. His uncaring and disrespectful behavior weakened their bond.

With a wounded self-esteem, Janice may have found herself facing two choices: staying in an unhealthy marriage while maintaining the status quo or removing herself from the relationship. She chose the later.

Janice left her husband and worked on herself. She came to know who she was and what was important to her. She learned to value herself. When Janice reunited with her husband, she was able to set clear boundaries and reinforce them. She no longer gave him permission to control her or be condescending. As a result, the dynamic of the relationship changed, increasing her marital satisfaction.

While setting boundaries is critical, it is not always the easiest thing to do. People who have a poor view of themselves often fail to set limits in their relationships for fear of being rejected or retaliated against. Because they do not feel worthy, they have difficulty demanding love and respect.

When we see ourselves in a positive light, we are able to assert our needs without experiencing intense fear of rejection and abandonment. It is when we feel inadequate and insecure about our lovability that we have difficulty finding a voice. We silently relinquish our power.

"I couldn't take it anymore"

Life With a Controlling and Abusive Man

In a healthy relationship there is a balance of power and control between the two partners. Both are able to relinquish some of their control, while standing up for their needs.

In relationships where an imbalance of power exists, one person has a chronic desire to be in control while the other person has difficulty asserting his or her own needs. This is what happens in an abusive relationship.

The emotional wounds we carry from childhood can make us vulnerable to experiences that cause us significant pain, such as being in a controlling and abusive relationship.

Kathleen, a forty-year-old school teacher, is married to a verbally and emotionally abusive man:

> My husband and I have grown apart, and I don't know when we lost each other. I don't feel we have a strong relationship, and things are getting worse.

My husband leaves home early in the morning and returns late every night. When I ask where he's been, he tells me he was with his friends. I sleep with my daughter, and I don't even know what time he gets home. I don't think he wants to come home.

Shawn barely speaks to me. He ignores me. I feel invisible to him. He doesn't spend any time with me or the kids. I think he's trying to avoid us. He calls me fat and ugly. He has been calling me names since our first child was born, seventeen years ago.

When we first met, everything was great. We were always together, and I felt attracted to him. However, as time passed, he became abusive toward me. I think I expected him to treat me like that because that's how my father treated my mother.

I no longer tell him how I feel because I don't want to upset him and fight in front of the kids. I hold it all in. How does that make me feel? Angry, hurt, and sad. I used to be a size three and now I'm fat. My counselor says that I'm depressed. I think he's right. For so many years I had hoped that my husband would change, but I know now that it's never going to happen. If I want things to change, I need to be the one who makes it happen.

I haven't left my husband yet because even though I make money, I don't know if I can pay our mortgage. My husband never wanted me to become financially independent. I was a housewife for many years before I decided to get my college degree. When I was going to school, he made it difficult for me. He took away my car, wouldn't help me with the kids, and made me cry before my classes. I would go to school with my eyes red and swollen. But I didn't give up. I graduated, and I'm happy for doing it.

I'm focusing now on bettering myself. I have a good job, and I'm learning how to be a better mother. I'm slowly getting my life back. I want to get strong enough to leave my husband. One day I'll walk away from my marriage, but I don't feel ready to leave him yet. I'm afraid of being alone, that no one else will want me.

Kathleen experiences rejection, abandonment, and deep hurt in her marriage. Her relationship lacks healthy intimacy.

Like Kathleen, Kimberly, 34, was also in an abusive relationship. As often happens, Kimberly's marriage crumbled in front of her and she reached rock bottom. Despite the deep hurt and pain, she was able to pull herself together and regain control of her life. She created a new beginning for herself. Here is her story:

I was twenty-five when I got married; one month after my first child was born. I got married without being in love with my husband. We were going to see how things worked out. We just took a chance.

As I expected, things didn't go well. Fred was never around, and that showed me that he wasn't in love with me. A man who's in love with his wife is going to be there for her and their children, helping out, helping one another. Fred wasn't physically or mentally there for me.

I think there was too much dishonesty on his part. Maybe he was dishonest with himself, what he wanted to do in his life. He was dishonest since the beginning. I should have taken those first clues seriously.

"Which clues?" I asked.

Well, when we started dating, I was working in a dental office. Fred would come over every single day and called me all the time. In one conversation, he told me that little lies were okay. I think he called it white lies; "White lies are okay," he said. I thought "Oh, look at this guy with an accent, he's still learning English and has no idea what he's saying." I should have known better. He was a liar from day one. He lied about everything. He lied so he could do whatever he wanted to do.

Despite all the lies, I married him, and soon after we had our first child. Day after day he was never there for me and the baby. He would always be at a friend's house. It was just about him; his life, his friends, and his enjoyment. When I would complain he used to say, "Well, I sleep at home." But I would say, "Where did you go all day long until nine o'clock? Where were you? I needed your help; we have a child!" But he didn't care about me or his child.

Four years into our marriage I gave birth to our second child. Our relationship was wearing down. We were constantly fighting, and I was feeling unhappy. I wanted to work, but Fred never let me have a job. I wanted to do something other than being in the apartment with my babies. He told me I couldn't work and that I had to stay home taking care of the kids.

One day I found little stamp marks on his hand. I found out that he was going to clubs. When I asked him about it, he put me down and made me feel fat and ugly. Honestly, it was a nightmare.

The emotional abuse lasted throughout the entire relationship, and it was the worst five years of my life. I put up with everything because I wasn't working. I didn't have money and I couldn't leave. I couldn't just walk out and get a place for me and my children. Also, I believed that the only reason a person should get divorced was if the other person was having a relationship outside the home. Of course, that was just around the corner.

We had been together for five years, when one day, I saw Fred with another woman in his car with their arms around each other. I confronted him, and he didn't deny having an affair. At that point I couldn't take it anymore, and I decided to leave him.

After we separated, I got a job right away. In the beginning it was hard. I had no family to help me, and Fred wasn't reliable. At times I thought I couldn't make it on my own. I was afraid of not being able to provide for me and the kids. I was also lonely. However, despite the difficulties of being a single mom, I felt an enormous weight had been lifted off my back. I no longer had someone calling me names and arguing with me all the time.

As time passed I slowly began to heal from the emotional damage that my ex-husband caused. I met my second husband who's different from Fred. He loves and respects me. He and my kids are the most important people in my life. I feel good about myself and how my life has turned out.

Kimberly, Kathleen, and many other women have been or are in a relationship with a controlling and abusive partner.

If you are one of them, you are probably familiar with the dynamic of the relationship. Your partner tries to control where you go and who you see; talks to you in a hurtful and demeaning way; ignores or puts down your opinions, and blames you for his abusive behavior. You try your best to make things work, but your relationship with him is far from intimate and satisfying.

His abusive and controlling behavior eventually takes its toll. You may realize you are no longer laughing like you used to and that you have lost some of your sparkle for life. You distanced yourself from family and friends—you feel lonely.

You notice feelings of resentment, anger, and hopelessness growing inside you. Slowly, you may lose your identity and start seeing yourself through his eyes. This person, who once promised to love and respect you, becomes that constant voice in your head, instilling doubt in your own value as a human being. He reinforces your feelings of fear and insecurity and takes advantage of your vulnerability until you surrender and lose faith in yourself.

But who is this abusive man?

He can appear charming to others, but behind this façade is a man who uses intimidation and control to mask his feelings of worthlessness and inadequacy.

He's a person who feels uncomfortable with intimacy and, as a result, is unable to develop a healthy bond with his significant other.

While he has difficulty emotionally committing to a relationship, he is unlikely to accept the end of one. He manipulates his spouse not to leave, and she feels held hostage in a painful reality that she endures longer than she desires. Where to go and who to turn to, often goes unanswered.

This woman is likely to have poor self-esteem and come from a family where she was not provided with a role model of a positive and loving relationship. She tends to hold some misconceptions of herself and intimate relationships. She may believe she does not deserve any better, that she is the cause of her spouse's abusive behavior, or that being alone is more painful than being in an unhealthy relationship.

Fear of retaliation, inadequate financial and emotional resources are often contributing factors in preventing such a woman from leaving an abusive relationship. Of course, when kids are involved, the decision to walk away can be even more difficult.

Staying in an unhealthy relationship, however, can be extremely detrimental to the children involved. Kids who grow up in abusive homes are prone to experience anxiety, depression, and anger problems that can ultimately lead to difficulties in many areas—social, emotional, psychological, and behavioral. These children are also at a greater risk of experiencing unhealthy intimate relationships later in life.

If you find yourself in a relationship with a controlling and abusive partner, you need to remember that his behavior is not an indication of his love for you, but rather of his fears and insecurities. True love is based on trust and respect, not control and intimidation.

The day that a woman decides to end an abusive relationship, she is giving herself a chance for a better life. If she works on reconnecting with herself and making positive choices, she will see that change can be an empowering experience, an incredible journey of self discovery, growth, and personal fulfillment.

"I lost my self-esteem"

The Power of Toxic Shame and Guilt

Every woman enters marriage believing it will bring her happiness. After all, she is living the fairy tale: the beautiful party, the ideal partner, and the prospect of a life full of joy, all within her reach.

For some women, marriage becomes a great source of contentment. They are able to develop a solid bond with their spouses, finding in them a friend, companion, and lover.

Married life, however, does not go well for everyone. As time passes, a great number of women find themselves unable to recognize the person they fell in love with. That same individual who once promised to love and respect them for eternity turns into a stranger, someone who slowly tries to take away their confidence, self-respect, and joy for life. In a hopeless state of mind a woman watches her dreams shatter and her belief in love slowly fade away.

Melissa, 64, shares about her difficult and painful marriage of forty years:

> When I began dating my husband, there was a strong mutual physical attraction. However, as time went by, I realized that we were completely different. I wanted love, affection, and respect. He wanted sex and no commitment. He would go out with other women and tell me at the same time that he wanted to marry me. I was naïve and believed in what he said.
>
> My intuition, however, would tell me that he wasn't in love with me. I also questioned my feelings for him. However, the sexual desire he expressed for me stimulated me to stay in the relationship. I thought that love would grow as time passed.
>
> I was 22 years old and had two previous romantic relationships before I met my husband that caused me a lot of pain and hurt. At the time I believed I would never find a man who would want to marry me. I was emotionally immature, and it was all the result of a traumatic childhood.
>
> When I was going out with my husband, I felt that he wasn't the right person for me. I tried several times to break up with him, but he would seduce me over and over again. I tried hard to be strong and not let myself get involved with him, but I ended up getting pregnant. I was desperate and didn't know what to do. Being a single mother was scary because I didn't have support from my family. I experienced a lot of fear and anxiety. I felt like dying.

After my husband found out I was pregnant, he proposed. I accepted, and it was the worst decision I ever made in my life. Soon after we married, he started neglecting me. He never encouraged me or made me feel good. I felt ashamed. That's how my family and his family made me feel. I felt guilty. I lost my self-esteem, and I was deeply hurt.

I tried to endure and find strength in the hope that, when our child was born, things would change. However, nothing changed. He didn't become more responsible or even more mature, as I had expected. I felt I was a burden in his life.

Time went by and I had two more children, always without him around. He never gave me love, affection, or a reason to be happy. He was a workaholic and womanizer. I was a housewife taking care of the kids. He liked to drink and be with his friends. Being with me at home was the last place he wanted to be. I felt lonely. We started fighting a lot. I began to demand that he become more responsible, and he would threaten to divorce me. This would intimidate me because I was afraid of not being able to support myself and the kids. The sadness and frustration I was experiencing was so overwhelming that I turned into an aggressive, bitter, and hostile person. I started to hate him for turning me into that and for killing all the feelings I had for him.

At a certain point in our marriage he stopped seeking me out for sex and was constantly hostile and aggressive toward me. Anything I said was reason for an argument or conflict between us. At times, however, he would withdraw. He would get home and go straight to sleep in another room without saying a word to me. He would ignore me. He said that he wasn't turned on by me anymore and that he wanted to divorce me. I suspected that he was having an affair.

A few days after he told me he wanted a divorce, I received an anonymous call from a woman saying that he had a mistress. I wasn't surprised, but I confessed I felt desperate. When he got home that night I talked to him about it, but he denied everything. I decided then not to talk about it anymore, not because I believed him, but because I knew that nothing would change. I was so tired of fighting to have a good relationship and failing that I gave up believing he could change. I started feeling depressed. I contemplated suicide. However, when I thought about my kids, I wouldn't have the courage to follow through. I didn't want to hurt and shame my family. I didn't want to make the same mistake I made when I was young.

Today we both are old. We need each other. When he doesn't drink, we get along well. However, when he comes home drunk, I have to be careful what I say because he hits me and says hurtful things. This is how I've been living the last forty years of my life.

It is not uncommon for women to find themselves in an unhealthy and unfulfilling marriage. Some wind up walking away while others don't feel empowered enough to do so. The fear of the unknown, of being lonely, or not having the means to provide for themselves and their children, can prevent women from taking such a bold step.

Melissa, like many other women of her generation, had to make critical decisions about her life at a time when society was not as empathetic and supportive of women's needs. As happened to many married women, Melissa found herself experiencing an unfulfilling marriage while dealing silently with hurt, fear, and guilt.

Women tend to carry a heavy burden on their shoulders, a tremendous weight that I call unnecessary guilt. We feel guilty about many things. For instance, we may feel guilty for thinking about ourselves first; for not being able to meet other people's expectations; for believing that we are failing as a mother or wife; or for having a strong desire to end a toxic relationship. Our tendency to excessively blame ourselves for things we can or cannot control leads us to experience anxiety, depression, and low self-esteem. We feel sad and unhappy.

While healthy guilt is important in helping promote acceptable behaviors, many of us experience guilt that jeopardizes our growth and well-being. Toxic guilt occurs when we take unfounded responsibility for things beyond our control. For instance, a woman may tell herself that it is her fault that her partner beats her. By holding such a belief, she is feeding inappropriate guilt and wrongfully believes that she can control her partner's behavior.

In addition to toxic guilt, a great number of women experience debilitating shame. This feeling causes people to see themselves as unlovable, flawed, and worthless. Those who experience chronic shame do not feel good enough in their own eyes and the eyes of others.

Our toxic shame and guilt have their origin in our childhood. Some of us had overly critical parents or were neglected and abused as a child. These early experiences made it difficult for us to develop an adequate sense of self-worth. As a result, we grew up believing that we are somehow defective and unworthy of love and acceptance. We become ashamed of who we are. Our debilitating shame and guilt play a major role in how we see ourselves and behave in our intimate relationships.

"I felt ashamed and guilty" and I will "never find a man who would want to marry me" is Melissa expressing her feelings of shame and guilt. These statements reflect how she feels about herself—inferior and worthless—which unfortunately is how many women feel.

Melissa's feelings of inferiority and inadequacy likely interfered with her ability to assert herself and solve conflicts in her marriage. It may have also made it difficult for her to give and receive love in a healthy way.

Some events in our lives can intensify our feelings of shame and guilt. For Melissa, it was her pregnancy. Melissa was unable to separate her self-worth from the mistake she believed she made by becoming pregnant.

Shame may trigger anger, which can lead to aggression. The emotional neglect and abuse Melissa experienced in her marriage confirmed her view of herself as unworthy and increased her feelings of pain and anger. In an attempt to restore her self-esteem, she may engage in aggressive and belittling behaviors. While behaving in such a manner provides her with momentary feelings of power and control, it ultimately distances herself from others. This leaves her experiencing rejection and abandonment, the same feelings she has tried to avoid her entire life.

Melissa failed to receive from her husband the unconditional love and acceptance that may have helped her overcome her feelings of inferiority and worthlessness. On the contrary, his behavior has contributed to her belief that she is unable to inspire love and affection.

Melissa had known for a long time that things should have been different. Yet, through all of this, she has maintained the status quo of her relationship, since change is a frightening road to travel. For so long, she has been hiding behind feelings of pain, guilt, and shame.

Like Melissa, many of us experience chronic feelings of shame and guilt and end up marrying a person who also views himself as unworthy and flawed. Healthy intimacy is not possible in such a relationship.

There are many of us who live unfulfilling lives because of our unhealthy shame and guilt. These powerful feelings underlie our intense fear of rejection, our feelings of anger and inadequacy, and our sense of hopelessness and helplessness.

To find inner peace, we must overcome these feelings. We do so by understanding their roots and how they are being reinforced. In this process of healing we ask ourselves some important questions:

"What events from my childhood or adult life does my shame and guilt stem from?"

"What are the fears, beliefs, and behaviors contributing to my shame and guilty?"

"Do I feel guilty for what happened to me in the past?"

"Do I feel I am not good enough to be loved?"

"Do I believe that I do not deserve to be happy?"

Once we identify our irrational beliefs, we challenge and replace them with positive statements and actions that bring us hope and strength. We work on accepting our mistakes as part of being human instead of seeing them as a reflection of our worthlessness. We make it a point to let go of our anger by forgiving ourselves and the people who have caused us pain. We say no to whatever and whomever is not good for us and pursue what is meaningful with the conviction that we have the means to do so.

"My mother-in-law shred me to pieces"
When a Mother Interferes With a Marriage

It is no secret our in-laws can have a major impact on our marriage. Some of us have a great relationship with our husbands' parents; in fact, our in-laws become our second family. Others, like Melissa, 64, are not so fortunate.

In the previous chapter Melissa shared about her disappointing and unfulfilling marriage. Here she talks about how her mother-in-law contributed to her marital dissatisfaction:

I'm afraid to talk about my mother-in-law because she's dead. However, she was the only mean person I met in my whole life. She was cruel to me. For many years she hated me because she thought I wasn't the right woman for her son. She blamed me for getting pregnant and being a burden in her son's life. She treated me like his maid. She would often show up unannounced at my house to check on how I was doing as a mother and housewife; if I was cooking, cleaning, and so forth. She would comment on everything and criticized me when I didn't do things her way. Basically, she wanted to control my life. She would also talk bad about me to my husband. He would get home angry and criticize me and put me down. She would tell me that her son wasn't happy and, if I wasn't happy either, it was my fault. She had plans for her son, and I ruined her plans. She wanted him to marry a wealthy woman from a prestigious family. I paid a high price for not being the person she pictured for her son. She was constantly trying to make me feel that I wasn't a good enough mother or wife. I started feeling sorry for myself.

One day, I'd had enough. After so much humiliation and pain, I had the courage to stand up for myself. I knew I had to protect myself against her. The lamb became a wolf. I kicked her out of my house and told her not to come back. I told her that I wanted to divorce her son, and I asked her to take him back to her house where he belonged. She left my house crying, and an hour later her entire family showed up at my door step trying to make things better. But seeing everybody there just made me angrier and more hateful of his family. I told them to get out of my house and to forget about me and the kids.

From that day on my husband's family began to respect me. I didn't see my mother-in-law for a while, which was great. When I started seeing her again, she no longer made comments about my life or criticized me. I noticed she was more cautious when she had something to say to me. She realized that she would no longer control me the way she once did.

Those were difficult times in my life. The pain and resentment that I've carried inside me has never gone away. I have bitter memories and wounds that will never heal. I never forgave what my husband's family did to me, just like I'll never forgive him. He took away my life and my soul. Only God knows and understands the pain I went through. He'll be there to comfort me when I leave this world for a better place.

Like Melissa, Brenda, 38, didn't feel accepted by her mother-in-law. She also didn't have much support from her husband:

Robert's mother is a true bitch. She did some horrible things while we were married. She shred me to pieces. One of my breakdowns happened at my ex-sister-in-law's house in San Francisco. His mother came up to me and said, "What have you done to my son? What have you done to him?" She went on and on. I was crying because I was just trying to be the good wife, and he was complaining all the time. He just sat there while I looked at him. I was thinking, why don't you help me out and tell your mom that it's not my fault? But he just sat there and let her do that to me. He took her side. He agreed with everything she said. I thought our family was his family, but it wasn't—his family was his mom and dad. He was the perfect son in their eyes. If he had to make the choice again, he never would have left his parents.

Robert and I were having problems in our marriage for a while, but what led to our break up was an episode with his mother at a restaurant to celebrate her birthday. We were all having lunch when I realized that she and Robert were playing with each others feet under the table. They were flirting with each other. Then something else happened. One night I walked into our bathroom where we have this huge bed, and I see Robert and his mom on the bed, with our baby between them. Robert never laid down with me and the baby. I guess I was jealous. I looked at him and said, "Why don't you just go fuck your mother?" I went ballistic and he said, "That's it, I'm getting a divorce and you need to get out of here."

Meeting a future mother-in-law is nerve-wracking for any of us. Will she like me? Will she think I'm good enough for her son? Will she accept me? These are all questions we are likely to ask ourselves.

Every woman wants to gain the affection, approval and trust of their mother-in-law. Most women tend to develop a positive relationship with their father-in-law, but when it comes to their husband's mother, they may find it's not always so easy.

Some mothers-in-law see their sons' wives as a threat. They may fear being replaced and excluded from their sons' lives. Their fear of rejection can lead them to resent and never fully accept their daughters-in-law.

When a mother fears losing the bond or power she has over her son, she is more likely to find that no woman is good enough for him. In an attempt to maintain control, she may intrude into her son's marriage and begin a long running battle with her daughter-in-law.

If your in-laws begin to interfere in your marriage, your partner's support is critical for the well-being of the relationship. Having your husband's support does not mean he will always take your side, but rather acknowledge your feelings and make decisions as a couple. If he decides to turn to his mother or both parents for help in making important decisions while at the same time excluding you, this can lead to marital conflict. Some husbands go as far as sharing the details of their marriage with their mothers, which can be upsetting for a woman. It feels as though a man forms an alliance with his mother, and his wife becomes the outsider. It's what his mother says and wants that counts, and any negative comments about her may not be well received.

If your partner allows his mother or both of his parents to have a say about everything in your marriage, it's likely that you will feel disrespected, betrayed, and rejected. This can cause your trust, respect, and love for your partner to gradually fade. When this happens, feelings of resentment, sadness, and isolation begin to grow inside you.

While it's important for a man to have a healthy relationship with his mother, some moms develop an unhealthy attachment. These mothers usually do not have any interest in seeing their son in a committed relationship. They are threatened by their son's love interest.

Have you ever met a man who has an unhealthy relationship with his mother? If so, this man likely came from a family where his father was physically and/or emotionally absent and his mother turned to him for support and companionship. This type of woman wants to keep her son close to satisfy her emotional needs.

The unhealthy relationship between a man and his mother can make it difficult for him to fully commit to a marriage. He feels trapped between his mother and his wife. When this happens, he will likely fail to meet his wife's need for love and support. This can lead a woman to resent her mother-in-law and attempt to weaken her husband's bond with his mother.

For a marriage to work, a couple needs to be committed to one another and set clear boundaries with their parents. It is important that they be in charge of their own decisions. If either set of parents feels the right to intrude into their child's marriage, the couple will need to work on establishing and maintaining appropriate boundaries. If they disagree on how much either set of parents will be involved in their marriage, they should resolve their differences by listening to each other and reaching a compromise.

Setting boundaries with parents should not be seen as hurtful or disrespectful, but rather as an indication of emotional health. When people have difficulty setting boundaries, it may be an indication that they have unresolved attachment issues. Problems in this area can prevent a person from experiencing a healthy and fulfilling intimate relationship.

"It all began with friendship"
The Extramarital Affair

All of us have been attracted to someone other than our spouses. Have you ever caught yourself thinking about a co-worker who is charming or a friend who takes the time to listen to you? Have you ever desired to feel the rush and excitement of falling in love all over again? If you have, you are not alone.

We all meet people to whom we are attracted, regardless of whether or not we are happily married. We may feel drawn to another person because of his kindness and intelligence or the attraction may be related to his looks and personality. While we may fantasize about someone other than our spouse, we may not necessarily act upon our feelings.

So, what does it take for a woman to remain faithful?

Moral and religious principles, fear of social disapproval, or fear of being discovered are likely to influence a woman's decision not to pursue an affair. However, the most important reason is how rewarding her marriage is.

Marital satisfaction is greatly linked to how desired we feel by our partner. The desire may not be primarily sexual in nature, but emotional. That is, we expect our spouse to show that he loves us by being supportive, loving, and respectful. We want him to work with us as a team by helping each other out. We don't want him to keep secrets from us or do anything that causes us deep pain. If this happens, we lose trust in him.

How desired does your partner makes you feel? If his desire for you is strong, you will likely be drawn to him and be content in your marriage. As a result, you are less willing to risk hurting your relationship for the novelty and excitement of an affair. The stronger the bond you experience with your spouse, the less vulnerable you are in seeking affirmation of your desirability outside the marriage.

Unfortunately, a great number of women do not feel emotionally close with their partners. In place of love and intimacy, there is a weak bond that no longer resembles the relationship they once experienced. Their partners' aloofness and often uncaring behavior comes across as a reminder that the connection that was once there is fading.

The disappointing turn that a woman's love life may take can lead her to contemplate an affair. Amy, a 36-year-old dentist, shares what contributed to her decision to be unfaithful:

I had been married for nine years when I had an affair. It all began with friendship.

Joe was my husband's best friend. He would come over to our house two or three times a week to hang out. My husband and Joe knew each other for many years. Joe was a single guy, about my husband's age. He'd never been married and didn't have other close friends besides my husband.

I liked it when Joe would come over and hang out with my husband and me. At times, however, I felt he was taking away my husband's time from me. I also felt my husband was enjoying spending time with his friend more than spending time with me. I talked with him about it, but things didn't change.

At the time my husband was going through a difficult time at work, and this was taking a toll on our marriage. We didn't talk as much, and we spent little time together. If he wasn't complaining about things, he would just sit quietly. If I asked what was wrong he would say, "Nothing, I'm just tired." He seemed unhappy all the time. I, on the other hand, felt sad and lonely.

Joe would usually come over before my husband got home from work. We would sit next to each other on the couch and enjoyed nice conversations. I felt comfortable talking to him about what I was going through with my husband.

Our first physical contact happened when we touched our feet accidentally. After a while we started touching our arms and eventually we were intentionally touching our feet and arms.

Joe wasn't handsome, but he was sexy. One of those guys who shows how much he desires you just by the way he looks at you. He had a sexy look in his eyes.

As time passed, we started flirting more and more, and my physical attraction for him started to grow. I started thinking about him all the time and got excited when I saw him.

Our next physical contact happened when I gave him a massage on my couch. Then we kissed. As our physical attraction increased, we no longer could hide it. We began flirting in front of my husband, and one day he asked if Joe was hitting on me. I denied it.

When the day came that Joe and I talked about our attraction for one another, we decided that nothing else should happen between us. That, however, just made our desire for each other grow stronger. He was in my mind all the time, and I fantasized about kissing, touching, and making love to him. Even though we talked about being only friends, it eventually happened.

My husband was on a business trip, and my child was sleeping at her friend's house. Joe called and asked what I was doing. I knew he wanted to see me, but was waiting for me to say something. I told him that my husband was on a trip. I had a few minutes to decide what I was going to say, then I finally asked if he'd like me to go over to his house. He said yes.

When I saw him at the door, I had mixed feelings. I was excited and turned on, but at the same time I was also feeling guilty. We sat down, had some wine, and talked for a while. He then looked at me, asked me to get up and grab my wine. He took my hand and walked me to his room. I was excited, but also scared and confused. I never thought I would have an affair, and there I was about to have sex with my husband's best friend.

The sex was great, maybe the best I ever had, but I felt guilty. I tried to block my husband out of my mind while at the same time thinking that his behavior led me to where I was.

After that night I became increasingly involved with Joe. We would see each other about once a week at his house. He started coming to my house less often.

It was hard to look at my husband's face after having sex with another man, but I was deeply involved with Joe, and it was too late to stop. Joe made me feel desired, sexy, and special. I felt he wanted me and desired me more than my husband did. Unlike my husband, Joe would get excited to see me, touch me, and spend time with me. When I was with Joe, I knew he was 100% there for me. I didn't feel invisible like I felt with my husband.

Joe and I were seeing each other for two years when things began to change. Joe started to become increasingly dissatisfied with how things were. He was the other man in my life, and this was probably hard for him to accept. Although we never talked about a future together, I think he wanted me to leave my husband. However, I had a child and wasn't ready to end my marriage.

My biggest fear became a reality when Joe started seeing someone else. He told me he liked her and was planning to get married. I was devastated. I knew he wanted a girlfriend, but I was hoping that day would never come. Also, I believed he was very much in love with me and wouldn't fall in love with anyone else. I was wrong.

It was hard seeing Joe falling in love and having to go through the pain of ending the affair. Joe had this new exciting person in his life while I was left dealing with the loss of the relationship. I think in the end, I got hurt the most.

When I look back I see why I let myself get involved with Joe. I was much in need of love, attention, and affection, and he was able to fill that void inside me at a time when my husband couldn't. I was extremely vulnerable when I met him.

While those two years were exciting, they were also stressful. I was constantly avoiding my husband, and I know he felt I was no longer sexually and emotionally interested in him. I felt guilty for betraying my husband and distancing myself from him.

While I was feeling rejected and sad with the end of my affair with Joe, I felt relieved. I would no longer betray my husband and I'd be able to invest again in my marriage.

Looking back, I'm glad that I didn't end my marriage. I know there's no such thing as a perfect husband, and I'm glad I never forgot my husband's qualities. I knew if I had divorced my husband and stayed with Joe, all that excitement would have eventually faded, the same way it did with my husband.

My husband never found out about my affair. Since it ended, my relationship with him has improved significantly. We still go through difficult times, but I'm glad we're together. At times I think of Joe. However, I don't have any desire to see him or have another affair. I feel good about myself knowing that I'm not betraying my husband. I do feel attracted and fantasize about other men, but I don't think it's worthwhile to act out my fantasies.

What do I think about extramarital affairs? I think that if you still want to be with your partner, it's not worth it. When we get involved with someone at an emotional and sexual level, we distance ourselves from our partner, and the consequences are immense. I learned that an affair is not only about excitement and novelty; it can also be a painful experience for everyone involved.

Anyone in a committed relationship will feel let down at times by a partner; no one is able to meet another person's emotional needs 24/7. We all have to deal with stressors in life, whether it is related to work, finances, family, or our own emotional issues. Being passed up for a job promotion, having a medical problem, taking care of a sick parent, or experiencing financial crises can greatly affect a person's well-being. Even less significant events, such as having a stressful day at work or at home with the kids, can influence how we feel. We may, for instance, feel more tense and irritable. Therefore, it is not every day that we have a smile on our face when our significant other gets home or vice-versa.

Since there are stressors we all need to deal with in our everyday lives, a couple should communicate well with one another to keep their bond strong and avoid unnecessary conflict. Open communication decreases the likelihood that one's behavior will be misinterpreted. For instance, your spouse may act distant as a result of problems at work. If you are aware of his problems and understand how he feels, you are less likely to interpret his behavior in a negative way.

When people make an effort to understand the source of their partners' undesirable behaviors and acknowledge that a majority of these behaviors are not intended to purposely hurt them, they may still be left disappointed; however, they are less likely to experience intense feelings of rejection, anger, or resentment.

There are situations when people purposely engage in behavior meant to hurt their significant other, which is usually a sign of anger and frustration. If the source of these negative feelings is not properly addressed, a cycle of negative interaction is likely to occur.

While difficult moments happen in every marriage, good times must prevail if a relationship is to succeed. In perpetual conflict there is discontent, hurt, and resentment. These feelings will eventually lead a couple to lose their emotional connection, making them vulnerable to act out on an attraction to another person.

When a woman feels disconnected from her partner she risks developing an emotional attachment to someone else. If she befriends a person who fills an emotional need that her partner is not filling, she may engage in an emotional affair that may become sexual. Remember that, unlike most men, women are more likely to become emotionally involved with someone before becoming sexually intimate.

But the key question a woman needs to ask herself is this: In the long run, is an extramarital affair worth it?

In an affair we can relive the wonderful feelings that we once experienced during our courtship with our spouse and the beginning phase of our marriage—the heart pounding, the feelings of bliss, and the rush of adrenaline. When infatuated, we experience a rush of brain chemicals that make us feel good. However, these chemicals don't last long. They wear off about two years into the relationship.

Infatuation is not the same as true love. Infatuation is just an illusion of being in love. When we are infatuated we perceive the object of our affection as our ideal mate, the person we see ourselves spending the rest of our lives with.

Anna, 41, describes how it felt when she was infatuated with her husband:

> He was such a nice guy. He was so gentle, he was so amazing. We had so much fun. He was the most beautiful thing I had ever seen. It was very physical; I thought he was the sexiest thing on earth. I used to call him my prince. He was so perfect. There was nothing wrong about him. We were so in love with each other. We couldn't wait to be together every day. I didn't care that he didn't have a good job or a lot of money. We had fun just being together. When I was with him, nothing else mattered.

When our relationship moves from infatuation to true love we no longer experience the intense physical arousal we once did, but have the opportunity to develop healthy intimacy with our partner. When this happens, other aspects of the relationship such as companionship, trust and emotional support, become extremely gratifying. These characteristics, as opposed to the euphoria we first experienced, can last forever and grow stronger as time passes.

Some people, however, do not ever get to experience true love. Their fear of rejection, abandonment, or failure makes it difficult for them to fully commit to a partner and develop a strong bond with that person.

Negative emotional states, such as anxiety and depression, can lead a person to become addicted to the emotional and physical experience of falling in love over and over again. As a result, affairs and ongoing involvement with new partners is likely to occur at the expense of true love and intimacy.

The allure of an affair can be seen by many as a way to "take care" of one's loneliness, sadness, or unfulfilling marriage. The relationship with a lover, however, is far from what mature love entails. In an affair, people are not exposed to their lover's shortcomings or the ups and downs of a committed relationship.

An extramarital relationship does not last forever and when it ends, a woman is likely to find herself having to deal with the loss of the relationship with her lover, as well as the unresolved issues with her spouse. The consequences on her marriage can be detrimental and irreversible.

When a woman chooses to have an affair, she might end up hurting herself more than she anticipated. She is risking carrying on an enormous weight of guilt and shame that can linger for years and cause great anguish.

We all have a choice in meeting our needs for love and intimacy in a mature and healthy way. An emotionally satisfying marriage or a monogamous relationship may not be as passionate and sexually intense as an affair, but it can bring comfort to a woman's soul.

"I fantasized that marriage would be an eternal honeymoon"

When Expectations Are Too High

A ll women enter marriage believing it will be an incredible journey. When they say "I do," they envision a future of happiness with the person they chose to be their life long companion.

With expectations set high, many women experience immense feelings of frustration and unhappiness upon facing the reality of marriage. For a number of them it becomes unbearable.

Debra, a 51-year-old business woman, shares about her disappointment with marriage:

> I've been divorced for three years, and I don't regret it. My relationship didn't work out because I had high expectations about marriage, and I got disappointed—it was all an illusion. It's not easy to share a life with someone, especially when two people have different temperaments and personalities. I hated having to put up with my ex-husband's habits. I had to give up a lot, especially my freedom. This triggered a

lot of disagreement, jealousy, and physical aggression between us. My ex wanted kids, and I didn't feel I was ready because my career was too demanding. As time went by I realized that the love and attraction we had for each other had faded. Nothing about him interested me anymore. When we talked to each other it was only to say what the other was doing wrong. I didn't accept the life I was living. When I left the marriage, I felt secure that I had made the right decision.

Amanda, 38, had her expectations of marriage crushed:

I've been divorced for five years, and I never expected it would happen to me. I thought I would marry the perfect guy and everything was going to be fabulous. We would talk about anything; it would be an intimate friendship and a spiritual journey. We'd be soul mates. If there was a problem he would say something sweet like, "Honey, you know another way to do this" and I would respond lovingly, "Yes, dear." Boy, was I wrong. Things didn't go as I expected.

Marie, 44, wasn't prepared for the challenges of marriage:

I believe that it doesn't help dating four, five, or six years to try to get to know the person you're going to marry. People only show who they are when they live together and have to deal with conflict, challenges, and frustrations. That's when the masks fall and they reveal who they truly are. People are usually surprised by what they learn from each other and many times disappointed. I think that the major difficulty married people encounter is not being able to deal with disappointments. That's because some people are too immature when they marry, and some fail to reflect on what it takes to make a relationship work. Also, a lot of women let themselves be carried away by the wedding party and the beautiful dress. Worst of all, they fantasize that marriage will be an eternal honeymoon. Unfortunately, that's what I did.

Like Debra, Amanda, and Marie, most women dream of living a fairy tale relationship. While most of us are able to experience a glimpse of that during courtship and the early stages of marriage, as time passes we are inevitably faced with the challenges that a life together brings.

Not all women deal alike with the reality of marriage. Some learn along the way that a true relationship has its hurdles and pitfalls. They accept that a marriage is made of great moments strung together through difficult times. The prince charming they dreamt of can never be found. While disappointed, they can still feel close to their spouses. They learn to embrace their flaws and admire their good qualities.

Some women, however, experience great discontent upon dealing with difficulties in a marriage. Their spouse's flaws become a source of great conflict and unhappiness. Convinced they can find their soul mates, they continue searching.

There are those women who decide to stay in a marriage hoping to change their partners to fit their ideal man. In their failed attempts, they experience frustration and resentment. When these feelings grow stronger, a woman is no longer able to acknowledge her partner's good qualities. This is what happened to Janet, 44, married for twenty years:

"Tell me one thing you like about your husband," I asked.

"Nothing," Janet replied.

We all experience some degree of disillusionment with our marriages because we tend to hold high expectations. Most of us picture ourselves with a person who is the complete package: a good provider who is also affectionate, thoughtful, faithful, and intelligent.

While our partner has some of these qualities, he will never meet all of our expectations, much in the same way that we will never meet all of his. We may, for instance, feel let down by our spouse for not showing his love the way we envisioned. Our partner, in the same token, may feel disappointed in us for failing to value and appreciate him. He may also feel deceived when he realizes that we can show a range of emotions that he was unaware of before the marriage.

We all want our marriage to bring us happiness, but we need to have realistic expectations. We should understand that passion eventually wears off and that it is important to work side-by-side with our partner to make the relationship grow. We need to be aware of and accept the fact that our significant other has flaws and will let us down at times, the same way we will let him down.

It is important to remember that many of the behaviors that we disapprove of in our partner will not change, but it is not because he does not care about us. People may rethink their values or change some aspects of themselves as they mature. They can, for instance, become more self-confident, grow closer to their families, become more spiritual, and so forth. Notwithstanding, their personalities will not change much. For example, if your husband is an introverted person he will not turn into an outgoing and extroverted individual.

For many of us, the prospect of living a happy life with someone we love is so exciting it doesn't leave much room to contemplate the challenges of marriage. No matter how much our mothers or other women try to show us what a marriage entails, we still believe in a fairy tale. The expectations are extremely high.

The higher the expectations, the more likely we are to blame our partner for our unhappiness. We may find ourselves thinking, if I'm not happy, it's because of him; he's not what I thought he was.

Having a loving and trustworthy partner is important to our well-being. However, when we exclusively blame our spouse for our unhappiness, we may fail to look inside ourselves and reflect on what we are doing or not doing to make the relationship work. Most of all, we may miss what changes we need to make in our own lives to bring about happiness.

At some point in her life Janet, 33, disconnected from herself. Her ever increasing feelings of insecurity and lack of personal fulfillment affected her marriage. Upon realizing that things were not working well, Janet decided to make changes. With conviction and determination, she worked on herself and got her life and her marriage back on the right track:

> When I first met my husband, I was self-confident. I was in college and had a nice job. I had a lot of friends. I was happy with my life. After we moved, however, everything started changing. I didn't have any friends and no work. I lost my confidence. I felt insecure. I began to like only what my husband liked

and only did what he wanted to do. I wasn't myself anymore. I didn't know who I was. Because I had been cheated on in a previous relationship, I was insecure about my husband's love for me. I was dependent on him. One day we had a serious conversation, and he told me that he didn't want to be my dad. He wanted me to be more independent. He also told me how much he loved me and that my jealousy was destroying our marriage. That was when I decided to make changes.

After doing some soul searching, I figured out what I wanted for myself. I opened my own business. I also started doing yoga and taking care of myself. These changes I made in my life helped me feel good about myself and strengthened my relationship with my husband. I learned to trust him and his love for me.

Our relationship with our partner affects how we feel about ourselves. Transversely, the way we feel about ourselves affects how we relate to our spouse. If you see yourself in a negative light or experience a sense of emptiness, you may have difficulty bonding with your partner. The same is true for him.

Since a healthy relationship with our spouse mirrors the relationship we have with ourselves, don't hang on to the illusion that finding your soul mate is the only answer to happiness. By doing so you may set yourself up for great disappointment. This faulty belief may prevent you from pursuing whatever could bring you happiness or, what I call, a sense of well-being.

If you allow yourself to believe that your happiness depends solely on finding the ideal mate, you are relinquishing your responsibility to make yourself happy. Unlike fairy tales, we don't need to be rescued, and we are not powerless, as long as we choose not to be.

A marriage can be a significant part of our lives, helping define who we are, but it should not be the sole purpose of our existence. Out of a fulfilling marriage we ought to expect a sense of peace and harmony to help us pursue what is meaningful.

We owe it to ourselves to find meaning in life. If we fail to do so, we may feel empty, sad, and hopeless. We are likely to experience anxiety and depression. When we feel depressed, we may have difficulty expressing affection, communicating well, and resolving conflicts in our intimate relationships. Instead of compromise, we are more likely to engage in verbal attacks, demands, and criticisms.

Unfortunately, some of us tend to feed into negative feelings and emotions that prevent us from finding peace within ourselves and seeing what the world has to offer. We are crippled at an emotional level, while at the same time trying to find happiness. We are searching for the wrong things in the wrong places. In our futile pursuit of happiness we feel tired, drained, and empty. We start seeing life as being unfair. We feel defeated.

Happiness is not a given. It takes self-reflection, determination, and courage to find meaning and joy in life. Through this journey we need to learn who we are, follow our hearts, and face head-on all of the obstacles along the way. If we do this, we are on the right path of experiencing what happiness is truly all about.

"My husband changed"

When Flaws are Revealed

The first years of marriage are fulfilling for most women. The majority of our expectations are met, and we feel fortunate for having found love. As time passes, however, the relationship we once believed was solid as a rock may begin to crumble before our very eyes. Marriage becomes progressively less fulfilling, and many of us blame this on the changes we see in our spouse's behavior. We may no longer feel as appreciated, respected, and loved as we once did.

Anna, 41, shares how her marriage changed from being a source of satisfaction to major disappointment:

> In the beginning everything was great. We spent a lot of time together. Sex was terrific. However, everything changed after we had our son.
>
> My husband is the only one who works. I'm a stay-at-home mom. I bust my ass every day, but I get no appreciation for it. He's never said, "Thank you

so much for what you do." The lack of appreciation is my biggest thing.

I feel sometimes like I'm walking on egg shells, when what I really want to say to my husband is: "You need to appreciate me more, you need to learn how much I do every single morning, every single day." I'm a good wife, and he never sees it. He never appreciates me. All I get is him saying that he pays the bills and stuff. I resent him for that. He's not the nice guy I knew and fell in love with.

One of the things I resent most is not knowing anything about his family's business. I'm afraid that he will take everything away from me. I feel insecure. I feel I don't have leverage. I don't have any ground. I have no money. I have nothing. I feel like telling him, "Who am I? Just the nanny you want to have sex with? Go find a whore!" I feel like I'm the mop that cleans the floor.

We no longer confront each other in front of our son. We just pussy foot around each other. We know now where not to go. I'm in my corner and he's in his corner. We're kind of living separate lives. We're basically roommates. There's no communication between us. When he's home, he turns on the TV and doesn't talk to me.

It's hard to live with my husband. Every day when I hear him pulling into the driveway after work I get anxious because I know he'll be bitching about his work and how miserable his life is. I'd like him to not be in such a negative mood. He's full of negative

energy, and I'm such a positive person. I choose to
be that way.

I don't think my husband is doing it intentionally,
but he's breaking my spirit. It's hard for me right now
to keep my spirit going. It's hard to be the cheerleader
all the time. I'm living such a phony life. I'm not living
the life I would like. If I didn't have my son, I would
probably have left my husband.

Like Anna, Maria, 42, experienced unforgettable moments
during the beginning of the relationship with her husband,
however, it didn't last:

In the beginning it was different. He was romantic,
affectionate, and thoughtful. He would open the door
for me, take me to places I liked, and surprise me
with flowers and romantic getaways. But everything
changed after we got married. Men do this. They
treat you nice just to get you.

During the early phases of a romantic relationship, a couple
strives to engage in positive behaviors to win the other person's
heart.

When the pursuit is over and the infatuation phase of the
relationship wanes, people may no longer feel the need to gain their
partners' affection. Therefore, they are more secure in revealing
their flaws and engaging in behaviors that the other person may
not like.

While a person's objectionable behaviors or traits are revealed
as time passes, some were present all along and may have actually
been a turn-on.

Diane, 42, married for eighteen years, found her husband's quiet and reserved behavior sexy and mysterious in the beginning of the relationship. However, as time passed, she began resenting these same behaviors:

> My husband and I worked together at a restaurant and that's where we met. I liked that he was quiet, respectful, and handsome. The mystery surrounding him was sexy. We dated for two years before we decided to marry. I loved everything about him. After we got married, however, I no longer felt the way I did. What I used to find attractive in my husband became a major source of conflict between us. His quietness was no longer exciting, but unattractive. His lack of interest in talking to me, in finding out what I was thinking or feeling, made me feel lonely and in need of attention. I thought my husband was going to be my best friend, but I was wrong.

Like Diane, 38-year-old Alice was married to a man whose personality traits were appealing; at least that's what she thought when she first met him:

> Before I got married I believed the right man for me had to be docile and sensitive with a good sense of humor. After many relationships I finally found someone who met most of my expectations. We fell in love and decided to live together. Soon after, we got married.
>
> The first few months everything went great. However, as time passed, his calmness, lack of initiative, and lack of ambition began to irritate me.

He wouldn't argue or talk much and generally found life to be wonderful.

He liked to sleep, read, play tennis, and would do everything I said. Everything was okay with him. It got to the point that I would provoke him just to see a reaction.

As time passed I became bored around him. His laid back attitude triggered anger and anxiety in me, and I began to resent him. I realized that I needed a man who was the complete opposite. Someone who would take initiative, stand his ground and vocalize his own opinions. I didn't want someone who would do everything I said. I asked for a divorce and, to my surprise, he agreed right way.

Some women experience increasing levels of marital dissatisfaction when they begin to resent some of their partners' behaviors that existed before the marriage, but were not major issues at the time. Often, these behaviors are magnified to the point that they become major flaws. This seems to be the case with Anna, 41, who has been married for thirteen years:

My husband has this thing of patting me on the back when I cry. It's so condescending. It's not even like a good real hug. He doesn't even touch me. He goes, "Come here." But I don't even want to because I know exactly what he's going to do. I tell him, "Oh, thanks. I could get that from my dog's paw." I get more love from my pet—it's so pathetic.

"Did he used to pat you on your back before you got married?" I asked.

"Oh, yes," she replied.

Anna says she dislikes her husband's habit of patting her on the back. She sees it as condescending. However, he used to engage in this same behavior before they got married, which more than likely did not affect Anna the way it does now. Her husband's intentions may be sincere, but Anna views his behavior in a negative light. Perhaps at this point in her marriage she wants him to show his love in different ways.

Anna may be going through what many of us experience. When we become infatuated, we either fail to notice our partner's undesirable behaviors or we don't let those behaviors affect how we feel about him. However, when the infatuation phase winds down, these same behaviors can become a source of great conflict.

During marriage or cohabitation, people inevitably show all sides of themselves, including the least desirable ones. This can lead couples to think they didn't really know their partners well. This is what happened to Cheryl, 52, married for twenty-two years:

> I was thirty years old when I got married. I had been dating my husband for five years. During that time our relationship was great. He was respectful, caring, and thoughtful. I thought I knew him well. I was wrong. We don't really know someone until we live with that person. As time passed he revealed himself to be a neurotic, sadistic, and cold-hearted womanizer. He likes to criticize me and say things to make me feel ugly and unattractive. He calls me a fat bitch and a cunt. I'm very unhappy. I'm doing my best; cooking, taking care of the house, and making sure he has everything he needs. But he's so critical all the time. Everything I do is wrong. Because I don't

work outside the home, he puts me down and throws it in my face that he supports me. I'd like to get a divorce, but I have two kids to raise. I'm afraid of not being able to make it on my own. I tried to look for a job, but I didn't find anything. It's going to be hard because I'm older, and I don't have a college degree. I'm hanging in there, but I don't know for how long.

Cheryl describes her husband as being thoughtful and caring during the first years of their marriage. As the years passed, he changed and became disrespectful and abusive.

It is possible that Cheryl's spouse had many good qualities, but changed over time. However, it could also be that when they were dating, Cheryl didn't see his tendency to be controlling or abusive. She may have actually been attracted to his controlling behavior because this was familiar to her. Her husband may have become more controlling as time went on, but his tendency to be controlling may have been there all along.

Like Cheryl, 38-year-old Brenda was married to a man who, over time, no longer resembled the person she once planned to spend the rest of her life with:

When I first met my ex-husband he seemed to be a very nice person. Bill was a little bit boring, but stable and conservative. I said okay, I'm 29-years-old and it's time to go for the nice guy. He was someone whom I saw myself spending the rest of my life with. However, to my surprise, he turned out to be someone totally different. As soon as we were married and I got pregnant, everything changed. Then everything I did was wrong. He became critical of me. I worked hard to try to keep everything together because of the kids, but nothing I did was good enough.

His behavior didn't affect me for long because I'm pretty resilient; I'm pretty strong. If he was complaining about something, I would just blow it off. I'd go with the kids to the beach, have a good time, and just try to keep things going. But I guess it was building up inside me. I was unhappy.

While many of us believe that our partner changed over time and is showing a side of himself that was unknown to us before, he may also feel the same about us:

"My husband tells me that he doesn't know me anymore," says Linda, a 42-year-old woman.

People may change how they interact with their partners over time, and this has a significant effect on the dynamic of the relationship. The way a person relates to a significant other brings about positive or negative responses, thus affecting the overall tone of the relationship. For example, if one person is often emotionally distant, the other may react by becoming critical. The emotionally distant partner may believe that his or her spouse has changed from being understanding and non-judgmental to someone who complains and is overly critical. This can lead to marital conflict and to a dysfunctional cycle of interaction.

Jean, 39, is caught in a negative relationship dynamic with her husband of fifteen years:

My husband keeps saying that I changed after we got married, that I'm constantly nagging and complaining. However, he's changed, too. We used to have a lot of fun together. We used to go out on weekends and spend time together. Now all he wants to do is stay home doing his own things. I feel like he's not interested in me anymore. He says that we need to save money, but when he wants to buy something, he goes ahead and buys it without even talking to me first.

Sharing a lasting and rewarding relationship with a partner requires emotional maturity, love and commitment from both parties. Marriage is not an easy ride. It has its ups and downs filled with moments of happiness and frustration. While some disappointment is inevitable, we should not allow ourselves to feel bitter and helpless about how things turn out. Empowered by a positive attitude, we should see marriage the same way we see life: a journey with rough roads to travel, punctuated by uplifting sights along the way.

"We don't listen to each other"

When Communication Fails

Every couple experiences conflict in their romantic relationships—after all, two people will never share the same exact interests, opinions, values, and beliefs.

Men and women, however, are not alike in how they address their differences. When a woman perceives that something is not going well, she wants to talk it over to make things better. She wants change. Men, on the other hand, are not as eager to talk about the relationship or making changes.

Elizabeth, 42, shares what her husband says: "Talking is a fairy tale. I don't believe in talking. My father never sat down to talk to my mother."

It is common to hear men say they do not want to talk because their wives just want to find things to argue about or that they are difficult to talk to. Some men also believe that talking is a woman's way of trying to change them.

What happens, however, is that when our partner is unwilling to talk, we feel defeated in our attempts to be heard. It's like he does not want to hear what we have to say. If what we say is not important, then we must not be important. At least, that is how we feel.

When our partner refuses, on a regular basis, to listen and validate us, we feel hurt, and our trust in him gradually fades. This is what Sarah, 37, experienced during her marriage:

> Greg wanted peace, he didn't want confrontation; didn't want to argue; he didn't want to deal with any emotions that I had. If I wanted to show or express them, he said he didn't want to listen. He told me that he only wanted to be around me if I was going to be pleasant, and if I was upset about something, he didn't want to deal with it. He would pull away. If I did talk about something that I felt upset about, he would always side with the other person; he would never try to understand how I was feeling. He would make comments like, "You're so defensive," but would never really try to listen to what I was saying. He thought I was making things up or that I was crazy. That made me feel hurt, and after a while I stopped trusting him. This guy doesn't even care; he's not being my partner, I would think.

Like Sarah, you want to be heard by your partner. But do you express your feelings in a constructive manner or do you blame your significant other and demand change?

When our partner withdraws and fails to validate how we feel, we may find no other option but to complain and nag. However, men or any person for that matter will react in a negative way when they are being blamed or criticized. A common reaction is to pull away.

We tend to nag and complain to express our frustration, resentment, hurt, and anger. Some of our complaints may not even be related to the underlying issue frustrating us. For example, if you feel rejected because your spouse doesn't spend enough time with you, and you've tried in vain talking to him about it, you may express your resentment by complaining about trivial unrelated things, such as the toilet seat that he leaves up or the mess he makes in the kitchen. However, when we complain, we risk being seen by our partner as hypercritical, demanding, and overbearing.

Maria, a 41-year-old housewife: "My first husband said I was too critical, but I think he never understood what I was complaining about. I think when people are in love, they can understand each other."

No matter who is doing the complaining, the person on the receiving end tends to feel mistreated and disrespected, which can lead to anger and hostility. A cycle of negative interaction and increased conflict is likely to occur. This unfortunate dynamic is present in many relationships, including Suzan's, a 39-year-old housewife:

"My husband complains about the way I talk to him. He tells me that I push him too hard."

"Push, how so?" I asked.

"That I always have something negative so say. However, I do get angry that he doesn't make time for me and the kids. He cuts me off and tells me he's busy. Instead of talking to me, he walks away."

Effective communication is critical in an intimate relationship. Therefore, men should be open to listen to their spouses, validating their feelings and reaching a compromise. Likewise, women should discuss their concerns without nagging, criticizing, or trying to change their partners.

Lisa, 46, and her husband communicate well with each other:

> Like most women, I believed in a fairy tale marriage. After I got married, my husband and I realized how challenging it would be. We decided we were going to work hard to make it happen. I've been married for twenty years and, like other married couples, we have conflicts and experience moments of frustration. However, none of our conflicts have been great enough to separate us.
>
> My husband and I talk about our problems and try to work them out without putting each other down. He listens to me and that makes me feel that he's committed to our marriage. I also give a hundred percent of myself to the relationship. I'm understanding and supportive. We remain close by recognizing when we're wrong and apologize if we're at fault. I don't ever want my husband to regret being married to me.

People at times behave in ways that causes pain to their significant other, even if that wasn't the intention. Therefore, when the situation calls for it, a sincere apology can prevent negative feelings from lingering and damaging the relationship.

Unfortunately, in a great number of marriages, including that of Nancy, 44, an apology is not always forthcoming when it is needed:

It makes me sad when my husband hurts my feelings and doesn't apologize or say he's sorry. I want him to apologize. If he says he's sorry, he's showing me that he cares about me and won't do it again. It turns me on sexually.

When our partner apologizes, he is telling us he is sorry for what he did or said. An apology can give us hope that things are going to change for the better. It also makes us feel that our partner cares about us and is invested in the relationship.

By the same token, we need to apologize when we are wrong or behave in a way that causes our partner pain. He expects to be heard and respected the same way we do. Like everything else in a relationship, an apology works both ways.

Listening to each other, apologizing, and expressing thoughts and feelings in an assertive way are critical to the success of a relationship. This, after all, is what effective communication is about.

Proper communication is essential for any conflict resolution and is in fact the core of a healthy relationship. So why is it that so many couples have difficulty in this area?

Not everyone knows how to communicate without being critical, judgmental, and demanding. People often point fingers at their partners and fail to listen and validate what they are saying or feeling. This ineffective pattern of communication is seen in many relationships, including that of 45-year-old Donna: "My husband and I have problems communicating. When we talk, it is to say what the other person is doing wrong. We don't listen to each other."

When people choose not listen to their partners they are behaving defensively, feeding their own anger and resentment. When this happens, understanding and compromise usually falls apart.

One of the things we must consider when trying to develop a healthy style of communication with our spouse is that men and women communicate differently. While it is important for us to share our thoughts and feelings and feel validated, men primarily use communication to solve problems. Therefore, they may fail to understand what we expect of them, and this can become a source of conflict.

When we share a problem with our spouse, it is likely he will not be interested in listening to us go on and on. Men do not like to talk just to talk; at least that is what they say. By talking, they feel they are not accomplishing anything. Instead, they want to help by offering solutions. That is how they feel they are being useful.

However, what all too often happens is that our spouse ends up giving us advice when all we want is him to listen and validate how we feel. We feel misunderstood when he expresses his frustration over how we handle things or when he is judgmental or critical of us.

Ineffective communication can be a major source of conflict in a relationship. For a couple to keep their bond strong, they need to listen to each other and express their thoughts and feelings in a caring and respectful manner. When lack of proper communication occurs, feelings of frustration and resentment are likely to surface.

Helen, 45, describes an episode with her husband in which a failure to communicate precipitated a conflict:

"I was so upset the other day with Matt. He got home and went straight to his room. He didn't even ask how my day was."

Helen went on to describe a conversation they had earlier that day:

"He called me in the morning and asked if I wanted to go out to have a drink after he was done working." I said to him, "Are you crazy? I'm not going out for a drink on a Monday."

"Did you find it unusual for him to invite you for a drink on that day of the week?" I asked.

"Yes. However, I found out the very next day that he wanted to take me out to celebrate our wedding anniversary, but I forgot about it."

"Do you think he might have gone to his room that night because he was hurt and upset with your reaction?" I probed.

"It could be," she replied.

The conflict that Helen and Matt experienced is common in intimate relationships. Let's take a look at what precipitated this episode:

Matt remembered their wedding anniversary and wanted to celebrate with Helen, but she rejected his invitation. Instead of talking to her about it, Matt walked away. Helen did not know what he was thinking or feeling and interpreted his behavior as rejection. Helen talked to Matt defensively when she turned down his invitation. Matt, on the other hand, responded in a passive aggressive manner by withdrawing. If both Helen and Matt had expressed their thoughts and feelings in an assertive way, there is a good chance they would have avoided this conflict or at least would have had the opportunity to address it early on.

Dialogue is another critical aspect of proper communication, and unfortunately it falls short in many relationships. When we talk to our partner, we do not want a one word exchange. We expect him to show interest by listening to what we are saying and sharing about himself. We want our partner to confide in us. When he reaches out to us, we feel valuable to him and a bond develops.

Isn't it hard when you perceive something is wrong with your partner, but he doesn't share? I remember as a child my mother asking my father what was wrong when he was quiet and unresponsive. He would always answer by saying that he was tired, a statement that is overused. It often means, "I don't want to talk." However, women do, and this can become a source of conflict.

Many of us have legitimate reasons for being frustrated by the lack of communication in our intimate relationships. While it is important to understand that our partner may not be ready to share his feelings with us at a moment's notice or that we will not have the kind of discussions with him we have with our girlfriends, we still need to converse with our spouse to feel close to him. If this fails, we may have difficulty seeing our partner as a friend and companion. As a result, we may disconnect from him.

Lisa, a 39-year-old teacher:

> I would get married again, but I'd marry someone who's more talkative. The lack of communication triggers a great deal of anxiety and loneliness in me. I feel that my husband and I are growing further apart.

Nancy, 52, believes men fall short in their attempts to communicate with their partners:

> Men have their basic needs: their families, their toys, and their hobbies. They also need other men's company, and when they try to understand women, it's difficult. When we ask them, "Can we talk?" it's like a wall. I don't know why they have such a hard time. Is it because they were taught not to cry and be strong? I believe men were taught to be warriors. They're the male. They're the strong figure and the provider, and to reach that emotional level without being feminine is difficult for them. They know about sex, but they don't know how we work. Men should be educated on how to talk to women and relate to them.

When two people really care and are investing equally in the relationship, they take the time to listen and understand each other. They are able to put some of their own needs aside and meet their partners half way. Nevertheless, if they no longer admire, value, and respect their significant others, they may be less willing to listen and compromise for the sake of the relationship.

In most of relationships outside marriage, be it with a boss, a friend, or a co-worker, people are able to find a balance between meeting their needs and the needs of the other person. For instance, people are usually quick to apologize to a friend when the situation calls for it, and they are aware of the consequences of behaving aggressively to a co-worker. However, when it comes to their intimate relationships, many have difficulty accomplishing the same goal.

Too often people feel increasingly comfortable with their partners and forget that love is not a given. When people only do what pleases them, they fail to show their significant others that they are important. Actions that convey love, if not present, will weaken the bond between two people. When this happens, the trust and emotional connection once there is inevitably lost.

"I feel worn out"

Experiencing an Unhealthy Marriage

With any broken heart, there is a story of love, betrayal, and loss.

When a woman enters a romantic relationship and commits to a partner, she is welcoming that person into her life. She opens her heart and expects the same in return. She makes plans and hopes for the best.

The path that a relationship takes, however, depends on decisions made by both parties. If one or both partners engage in behaviors that prevent them from connecting with one another, they risk causing irreparable damage to the relationship.

Ashley, 51, shares the story of her broken heart and the bond that she lost:

> I was married for ten years. My husband was married two times before, which should have been a sign. However, he made it clear that he wanted to be

my husband ten years before he finally married me, so I felt he really cared about me.

The first years of our marriage were wonderful. We went on trips and had a great time together. He was my best friend. He talked to me, gave me advice, and kept me strong when I was weak.

However, that all ended when he began using drugs. The drugs became the number one thing in his life and his friends number two, since they were his suppliers. I would work all day and, when I got home, his friends were there. I told them they were ruining my marriage, but they didn't care. I felt lonely and totally rejected and betrayed by my husband.

We started arguing a lot. He would say that I lectured him and that I was too strict—a mother type, he said—too controlling. But all I ever wanted to know was why he changed and why he wasn't the same with me. He no longer showed that he cared about me. I felt abandoned. I asked if he wanted to go to marriage counseling, but he refused.

My career wasn't as successful as it could have been because my attention was totally focused on my personal life. I was constantly afraid of what was going on in my house when I wasn't there. Am I going to be implicated and taken to jail because my husband is getting arrested? Are people watching my home and stealing from me? All these thoughts were going through my head. I was living a nightmare. I felt tired and drained.

I often asked myself, am I doing something wrong? Is it my fault? What can I do better? How can I make this up to him? I was questioning myself until I got to the point that I looked at my husband and said, "If you don't start making an effort to be with me then I think our marriage is over. We don't have a mutual commitment to each other. I'm the only one who is committed to this relationship and that is not what we promised one another."

Despite my pleas, he didn't change. I was feeling hurt and rejected. I was dealing with abandonment and the loss of trust in someone who used to be my best friend. I struggled with my feelings until I got to the point that I couldn't live like that any longer. I picked myself off the ground and moved on with my life.

I got myself a place to live, but I still visited my husband and talked with him all the time. Meanwhile, he moved other people into his life, and that was hard for me to deal with. I was in so much pain that I decided I had to take a break from him. I called him and said I was moving away. He wanted to meet. We had dinner together, and he asked me not to leave. I decided to give it another shot.

I moved out of my apartment and back in with him and his family. We were living together for a year when we made plans to move to Alaska. I quit my job, sold my car and my possessions. But while I was taking care of things, he got his money and left. I became depressed. I knew then we'd never get back together, that I'd never be able to trust him again. I realized that the drugs changed him and things would never be the same.

For such a long time in my relationship I felt I was being abused, and it was ruining me. It's almost as bad as the drugs. You never really get it back because physical abuse and mental abuse are two different things. However, they're also similar, and sometimes you don't know which hurts more. It's like, what's killing me more? Would I rather be hurt and get well fast or would I rather be changed psychologically?

During the last years of my marriage, I felt that my psyche and my entire core were slowly being eaten away. My soul was slowly being killed, like a fire burning itself out. It took its toll on me.

Being abandoned, betrayed, and misled has been extremely hard for me to deal with. I feel worn out after picking myself up so many times. I no longer get excited about things. It's not a fear of failure; I'm just tired. I'd like to get my spark back, but I don't know how to do it. I pray so hard every night for an answer. I think I'll have to dig deep into my soul and just make it happen.

I feel better though that I'm no longer on the verge of a dangerous breakdown. I'm blessed that way. The relationship was dragging me down, and I could no longer sacrifice my well-being. I needed to get my life back, even though at times it came back in pieces.

I'm starting to heal, but I still feel sad at times. It's like someone has died. When the person you've lost is alive, it's more difficult to mourn because the person can come back. You have to go through that pain again because you have this love for someone, even though it's not a healthy one.

When I go through the psychological thing of missing my ex-husband, the angel in me says, "Look at what he did to you. Look where he took you. Look where he left you. So how can you love him?"

It definitely helps to think that way, but you still take the same person you are today with you, no matter how far you go. We take the same suitcases. We need to repack our things, train our minds to go on to exciting new things. We need to create our own trip and wherever we go, it'll be okay.

Ashley fell in love, got married, and lived unforgettable moments. She was able to find in her husband a friend, a companion, and a lover. Yet it didn't last long. At a certain point in her marriage, the same man she once felt so close to slowly drifted way.

While feeling hurt and rejected, Ashley didn't give up easily on her marriage. She kept her hopes alive that things could be the way they once were. Despite her best intentions, Ashley eventually had to face the reality she so much tried to avoid—the end of her marriage. Devastated, she was left dealing with an immense sense of loss.

We all experience difficult times in our intimate relationships. However, when they occur too often, we are likely to find ourselves questioning whether the person whom we once believed was our soul mate is in fact right for us.

Regardless of our frustrations, doubts, and perhaps regrets, we don't walk away from a relationship without trying to fix it first. We hold on to the hope that things will get better.

While valuing and investing in our relationship is important, the desire to make things work at any price can be detrimental to our well-being. This is usually the case when we become emotionally dependent on our partner to the extent we end up abandoning ourselves for the sake of the relationship. In such cases we risk becoming co-dependents.

In a co-dependent relationship, we may take on the role of caretaker and try to please our partner at our own expense. Our spouse becomes the sole focus of our life and we feel an excessive sense of responsibility for that person's well-being.

When we are co-dependents we may have a need to control everything within the relationship. But at the same time, we are unable to assert our own needs or even acknowledge we also have the right to have needs. Our ultimate goal is to gain love and approval and avoid rejection and abandonment at all cost. In the end, we may end up feeling angry and hurt for not being appreciated. We are unable to receive from our partner what we fail to give ourselves—love and respect.

Which women are most susceptible to becoming co-dependents?

Co-dependency is a learned behavior that has its roots in a person's dysfunctional upbringing. Many people grew up in a home where there was alcohol and drug addiction, mental illness, and physical, emotional, or sexual abuse. Anyone raised in such an environment may fail to feel unconditionally loved and accepted. They were not often given a voice and therefore couldn't be heard. Consequently, they grew up carrying deep hurt, anger and shame. These feelings do not go away with time; instead, they become part of a person's life and often underlie the excessive use of alcohol and drugs, indiscriminate sexual activity, and involvement with unhealthy partners.

A co-dependent relationship can be detrimental to anyone. Many women whose partners have an addiction may find themselves in such a dysfunctional relationship. Their spouses tend to be needy, emotionally unavailable, and unreliable. These women feel the urge to rescue their mates while sacrificing their own needs. While they feel victimized, they are unable to break away.

Our unresolved emotional issues can lead us to pursue and maintain unhealthy intimate relationships. The emotional damage that such a relationship can cause may take a long time to repair, just like the wounds from our childhood. However, if we choose to do so, we can heal and move forward.

The way we start a new life is by "repacking our things," as Ashley put it. That is, we need to get in touch with our feelings, learn from our experience, and forgive the people who caused us pain. We need to take control of our lives by knowing where we want to go and who will be walking that road with us. With a new mindset, we embark on a new journey, a new beginning that allows us to gain back our spark.

"My husband cheated on me"

Being the Victim of an Extramarital Affair

One of the most heartbreaking ways to violate a person's boundaries is through infidelity. The hurt of being betrayed is intense and profound, and the process of recovery is long and painful.

Sarah, a 37-year-old mother of three, is one of many women who went through this ordeal:

> My husband seemed unhappy for such a long time, especially for the last four years of our marriage. A few years ago he started playing music. It's like he wanted to be a rock star. He regressed to being a teenager. Even though he's talented, he was always insecure about his music. I tried to encourage and support him. But that's how the affair started, with his music thing.
>
> Joe was in a band, and my best friend, Lisa, was the singer. I encouraged them to perform together. That was my biggest mistake. Playing music gave them

a chance to spend time together and get close to one another. As they started seeing each other more, my kids and I noticed they were flirting. I didn't want to even think they were having an affair because she was my best friend and he was my husband. I couldn't possibly believe that my husband and my best friend were sleeping together. However, my gut was telling me something was going on.

My suspicions were realized when I saw something that shook my entire being. I felt like my whole world was collapsing around me. I was in our house watching TV, the kids were in bed and everything was quiet. Joe was in the studio behind our house working on his music. As I was getting myself ready for bed, I heard him talking with someone on the phone. I walked outside and saw that the lights in the studio were on. I stopped to listen who he was talking to. What I heard at that very moment disgusted me. My husband was telling my best friend that he had a hard on. I peeked inside and saw him masturbating while talking to her on the phone. A few minutes later he told her that he had to turn down the lights because he didn't want to be seen. He continued masturbating and having phone sex with her. I stood outside the studio frozen, not believing what was before me. I was so furious I was shaking. How could my own husband be doing this to me? I stormed into the room and he hung up the phone. He was such a jerk. Instead of apologizing, he started yelling at me for listening to his conversation.

When I confronted both of them, he denied having an affair with her, and she actually had the nerve to say the phone thing was a "funny incident." I was confused, not knowing what to think. I was in denial.

I prayed to God and the universe for guidance, and a few weeks later my friend from Utah gave a call. It turned out she knew someone who was friends with Lisa. Lisa told that person she was having an affair with my husband and was madly in love with him.

I'm the complete opposite of Lisa. When Joe first met Lisa, he hated her. He would comment on how she was late picking up her sons, how she fed them sugar, and how her house was a disaster. He said I was responsible, dependable, and caring, and she was a complete flake compared to me.

Two months passed since I found out about their affair. In the beginning, when I saw her on the road, I would glare. But after a certain point I just decided to let go. I no longer showed any reaction at all. I noticed that when I started ignoring her, Joe changed. He didn't go to her house as much and things started to cool down between them.

It's still hard for me to believe that my best friend had an affair with my husband. She stole him from me and broke up our family. She didn't even care that our kids were best friends.

I used to tell her everything about Joe; things I didn't like about him and the problems we were having. I found out later that she told him everything I had said. She acted like a friend to Joe, listening to him and making him feel good. He took care of her, and she gave him lots of sex.

I feel hurt inside. I wish I had at least gotten support from his family. Joe's mother has shown no compassion at all during this difficult time for me and the kids. I resent her for that. When I found out that Joe was sleeping with my best friend, I went over to her house and asked if she knew her son was fucking Lisa. She looked at me and said, "All I know is that you and Joe are getting a divorce." She said that she didn't want to get involved. She also asked what I thought I could have done differently, implying that it was my fault he was having an affair.

Later I found out she invited Joe and Lisa to her house for dinner, not once but twice. I felt so betrayed. Joe and I are still not divorced. I'm working my ass off and taking care of his children, and she's inviting that woman for dinner. She doesn't find anything wrong with her son having an affair in front of me and the kids.

Right now Joe is living in the back of our house with his parents. His mother washes his clothes and cooks for him. She picks up after him, and everything he does is great. At sixteen she kicked him out of the house, and now he has a chance to be mom's little boy again.

Joe still denies the affair. He still comes to the house and tells me that if I want to get back together, he'll always be there. But will he really? Or only if I fit into his lifestyle—his paddling, his music, his parents, and Lisa. I told him if he wanted to get back together he couldn't ever see her again, but he couldn't even agree to that.

I decided that I need to move on with my life. I'm looking for a place for me and the kids. It's too hard to live with Joe on his terms, which has been the case since we got married fourteen years ago.

Like Sarah, Denise, 39, had to deal with infidelity and the end of her marriage. Here she shares about discovering her partner's affair, the deep secret she revealed to him, and life after the break up:

I met my husband when I was fifteen years old. Alex pursued me for a long time before I gave him a chance. At the time I had just broken up with a guy whom I was madly in love with. I found out he was cheating on me.

Soon after I started going out with Alex, he moved in with me. Even though I wasn't in love with him, I decided to invest in the relationship. Three years later we got married and moved back to my home town.

Alex worked for my father, and I was teaching. We never had financial problems, and my parents were always there to help us with our two kids. Everyone would comment on how much Alex loved me. I never felt insecure about him. He was a devoted husband and father.

While I felt that he loved me, I honestly couldn't say the same about my feelings. There were things about him that irritated me, and I didn't hide it from him. I didn't like his lack of ambition, his personality, or his family. Often I would tell him how much I disliked these things and the fact that he didn't make enough money.

A few years ago I met a guy at the gym. He was charming, wealthy, and had a great personality. I fell head over hills for him. Alex became suspicious I was seeing someone and started following me. He didn't find out about the affair, but it had a tremendous impact on our relationship. I become even more irritable toward him and wasn't interested in sex. I didn't want to leave Alex, but I also wanted to have someone else on the side. I wanted them both.

My affair lasted two years. During that time Alex began to change. He was no longer trying to please me. He began talking back to me. He was less patient with me and the kids.

Last year I got suspicious he was having an affair. He'd tell me that he had meetings after work and grew cold and indifferent. When I realized he'd changed, I tried to get close to him, but I guess it was too late.

One night, about seven months ago, I was spending the weekend at my parents' house at the beach when he called me around midnight. He told me he'd met someone and that he didn't love me anymore. I couldn't believe what I was hearing—my husband was saying he was cheating on me and was planning to leave me. I felt like the ground opened up beneath my feet. I never expected he would do that to me. We talked for a few more moments, then I hung up the phone, got my keys, and drove home. My father came with me. The entire two hours it took us to get back home, my dad and I didn't say a word. I felt like I was living in a nightmare and that I would wake-up and everything would be okay. I was desperate, confused, hurt, and angry. How dare he do this to me? I always thought I would be the one to decide if the marriage would end. I was wrong.

When I got home Alex told me everything about his other woman. It was actually someone I knew from the gym who's also married with two kids. He said they both agreed that night to reveal to everyone that they were seeing each other. He threw in my face everything I had done to him over the years; how I put him down and didn't value him. He told me he loved me so much, but that I destroyed all his feelings for me. He went on to share the details of his affair; where and when they used to meet and how long they had been seeing each other.

I started thinking about all those nights that he told me he was in meetings for work, when he was actually fucking her while I was at home taking care of our kids. I was so upset that I ended up telling him about my affair. I told him that I also fell in love with someone, but unlike him, I decided not to end my marriage. He got extremely angry, but didn't leave me right away. Worse yet, he decided to stay and torture me.

As the days passed, I got depressed. I didn't have the energy to do anything but cry. I lost a lot of weight and almost lost my job. Every day Alex was colder and more indifferent toward me. He didn't care that I was crying all day long and not eating. Some days I was nice to him, but others, I would remember everything he did and we'd end up fighting. I couldn't let go of what he did to me.

It had been four months since he told me about his affair, when one night I was feeling so depressed that I took a handful of sleeping pills. My mother came over and took me to the hospital. She told Alex to pack and leave before I came back home. It was extremely painful when I went back home and realized he was gone.

I've been on my own for six months now. My kids and I have been going through a lot of pain. I guess I'm paying for everything I did to him. I'm trying to rebuild my life, but it hasn't been easy. I've been going to work, and during the week things aren't so bad. The weekends, however, are depressing. I'd rather be with him cheating on me than to be alone. Even if Alex wasn't much of a talker, he was always there. Now I have no one.

I carry a lot of anger and hate for Alex. I can't forgive what he did to me and the kids. We still see each other at times, but when we do, we usually get into big fights in front of the kids. Now he doesn't even answer my phone calls. His girlfriend keeps calling me to say they can't be happy because of me and my children. I'm taking it day by day. It's going to take a long time to get over it.

Finding out about a partner's infidelity is incredibly disheartening to any woman. Wobbly legs, a pounding heart, and a turning stomach are some of the physical symptoms we are likely to experience. Anger, shock, and confusion are also a part of this painful discovery.

In addition to a range of physical and emotional responses, we may also find ourselves asking in disbelief: Is this really happening to me? Was my marriage a lie? Will I ever be able to forgive my partner? Did my marriage end? Where did I fail? Will I be able to trust anyone ever again?

Experiencing a satisfying intimate relationship is extremely important to all women, and we work hard making it happen. This is why it is difficult for us to deal with the end of a marriage. This is especially true when it occurs in the context of infidelity. The pain, hurt, and anger can be overwhelming.

No one is immune from becoming the victim of an affair. If it happens to you, you need to comfort yourself instead of becoming your own worst enemy. You shouldn't question your attractiveness or your desirability or compare yourself to your spouse's lover. If you find yourself asking questions like: What is it that I don't have that she has? Is she prettier, smarter, or more interesting than me? You may risk questioning your own worth and lovability.

"She listens and understands him, makes him feel good and gives him lots of sex" is what comes to Nicole's mind when thinking about Joe's mistress. Is Nicole comparing herself to her husband's lover and believing that she failed as a wife? Is she blaming herself for his affair? If she is, she will end up questioning her self-worth.

If you become the victim of an affair, don't be too hard on yourself! Don't make the mistake of taking responsibility for your partner's behavior or engaging in negative self-talking that makes you feel inferior. Also, don't count on restoring your wounded self-esteem by changing your appearance. Think carefully before you decide to undergo a makeover with the goal of "fixing" something to be accepted and reassured of your own desirability.

It is not because of your small breasts or a few extra pounds that your spouse was unfaithful to you. There are many husbands who have gorgeous wives, but cheat on them anyway. It is not by changing your looks that you will find true love. There are deeper issues other than your appearance that increase your chances of experiencing a healthy and rewarding intimate relationship.

The crisis in your marriage is not a direct result of your weight or any other physical feature. Instead, it is related to how you and your partner interact with each other, which in part is based on how both of you feel about yourselves. For example, you may have past unresolved issues that cause you anger, pain, or difficulty trusting. This in turn may affect your weight and your emotional well-being, thus interfering with your ability to bond with your spouse. Likewise, your significant other may have his own emotional issues that interfere with his ability to emotionally commit to the marriage and develop a connection with you.

If you find yourself experiencing infidelity in your marriage, it is critical that you take an honest look at the relationship regardless of whether you and your partner decide to stay together. Reflect on where it went wrong and what you could have done differently. Nevertheless, stay away from blaming yourself for his decision to be unfaithful.

Most marriages do not survive an affair, but there are couples who are capable of building a stronger bond. If you and your partner are willing to work on the relationship, you must allow yourself to trust him again. Once trust has been broken, it is difficult to restore.

The experience of being betrayed can lead you to build a wall, which serves as a barrier to protect yourself from getting hurt yet again. This self-protective shield, however, can hurt your chances of reconnecting with your partner and moving forward with your marriage.

While restoring trust in a relationship is critical for reconciliation, forgiveness is just as important, regardless how the marriage turns out.

The decision to forgive your partner should not be based on whether or not he deserves to be forgiven. You are not doing it for him, but yourself; for your own healing and inner peace. When you forgive, you are letting go of anger and resentment, the same feelings that can turn you into a bitter and unhappy individual.

If you are not willing to forgive, but instead hold a grudge against your spouse, you won't be able to trust him again and, most important of all, heal from this painful experience. You will continue experiencing deep sadness and anger. As a result, you and your partner will grow further apart and eventually fail in your attempt to reconcile.

As we all know, few marriages survive infidelity, and divorce is never an easy process. For many of us, a divorce represents the loss of the family unit, which can bring about an emotional response similar to death.

Therefore, during this most difficult time, it's okay to cry, be angry and deeply saddened. After all, you are grieving the loss of a relationship you once cared deeply about. Grieving will allow you to heal and bring closure to this difficult and painful time in your life.

It is important, however, to grieve the relationship you had with your former spouse and not the one you idealized for yourself. In other words, if you remember only the best moments of your marriage or how you wanted it to be, you will not allow yourself to grieve the relationship as it was. Your unrealistic view of your marriage will make it difficult for you to relinquish your attachment to your former spouse and begin a new life for yourself.

During the early phase of divorce it is common to experience an emotional attachment to a former spouse. You may think about him often or have a strong desire to see or talk to him. You may also catch yourself contemplating reconciliation. All of these reactions can occur despite the fact that you may hold negative feelings toward him or have a conscious desire to move on.

While a great number of people still feel emotionally attached to their former spouses after a divorce, eventually most of them break away. During this process it is important for you to spend time with loved ones and confide in those you trust. You should also pursue what makes you happy. This could lead to new things you have always wanted to do.

While you may fear the future of a life without a partner, do not allow this fear to grow inside you and trick you into believing you would be better off in an unsatisfying marriage. Likewise, do not hold onto anger and resentment; it will consume your life and intensify your pain and hurt.

Look at your divorce as a chapter in your life that is coming to a close and that you are putting behind you. A lot of women have been in your shoes and were able to rebuild their lives. During this difficult time, remember to stay away from negative thoughts; they can affect how you feel about yourself and your attitude toward life. Instead, welcome optimism and hope. They will take you on a path of learning, growth, and fulfillment. Look ahead; after all, this is where new and promising things are bound to happen.

"My life is so much better"
When Divorce is a Good Thing

Divorce is an especially difficult time in a woman's life. Sadness, loneliness, anger, and guilt are some of the feelings that are likely to fester during this painful experience.

Malia, 39, shares how this process has been for her:

> I've been divorced for two years, and it's been the most painful and difficult time of my life.
>
> My ex-husband and I used to fight a lot. He was abusive and unfaithful to me. I know I did the right thing to leave him, but I don't think I was prepared to be on my own with two kids.
>
> I have full custody of our children. Being both mother and father to my kids has taken its toll on me. I don't have many close friends, and my family doesn't live near me. I've gained a lot of weight since my divorce, and I'm not as financially comfortable as I was.

While I'm still struggling to get my life back on track, my ex already rebuilt his. It's unbelievable how men can move on so easily after a divorce. My ex is dating and seems content with his new life. What upsets me the most is that he has little time for our kids. When he does spend time with them, he brings his girlfriend along.

Unlike my ex, I haven't dated since our divorce. I met a few guys, but none worth having a relationship with. Part of me would like to meet someone, but the other part feels scared. I'm not sure if I can trust another man again. I feel lonely and unsure of what to do with my life.

No woman will ever be fully prepared to deal with a divorce. The end of a marriage is a major event in a person's life that can bring about great emotional distress. Despite the deep pain and sorrow, time is always a good ally. It allows the negative feelings to subside and eventually gives way to peace and harmony.

Brenda, 38, shares about her life after divorce:

Oh, my life is so much better. You just need to get yourself together slowly. It takes a long time, though. You have to stop and think what you're going to do. You have to be careful and separate yourself emotionally. You have to work on that, especially in the beginning. Be careful not to think, Oh, maybe we're going to get back together. I had a little bit of that, but it didn't last too long. And suddenly, after a year, two years, you look back and think, this is great now.

I've been divorced for three years, and things are going great. My kids have become the focus of my life. We've been so happy since the beginning, even when we didn't have any money. I prefer being poor, but happy and free. Just being able to come home to our place and not being criticized or mentally abused is wonderful. I have a life again. Finally, I'm getting back to being the person I was.

Like most women who go through divorce, Brenda was able to rebuild her life. While she has regained her joy, she may still carry the remnants of a relationship that caused her a great deal of pain. Here Brenda shares how marriage has affected her:

"My marriage changed me. It made me afraid of people, especially guys."

"Afraid of getting hurt?" I asked.

"Just afraid of getting close," she replied. "It's kind of sad to say, but I don't miss being with someone because I have so much going on with the kids. I'm focusing on other things. Maybe I'm just ignoring the problem or something."

When a woman commits to a relationship, she expects in return to be loved, respected, and honored. When this happens, she will develop a strong bond with her significant other and be content in her marriage. If, instead, her partner becomes increasingly controlling and abusive, she will disconnect from him. In this case she will have little chance of experiencing a gratifying, healthy relationship.

A woman often stays in an unhealthy relationship longer than she desires. When it ends, the pain gradually subsides, but the fear of getting hurt once more may linger. Once this fear grows deeper, a normal reaction might be to protect one self by "ignoring the problem," as Brenda put it.

The actual "problem" can be traced to an unstable self-esteem. When we do not feel secure about our self-worth or lovability, we anticipate being rejected and hurt. We may have difficulty demanding that we be treated with love and respect. Failure to set boundaries contributes to our relationship dissatisfaction and fosters a belief that it is unsafe to be in any romantic relationship. We become afraid of trusting a partner as well as ourselves.

The fear of being hurt yet again may lead us to continually avoid romantic relationships, long after our marriage ends. The price we pay for doing this, however, is extremely high. We are depriving ourselves of love and intimacy.

Instead of skirting love, we should empower ourselves by believing that we will not accept anything that is not good for our soul. We need to put into practice our right to say no to whatever or whomever causes us pain. That means saying no to a relationship that lacks respect, honesty, and healthy boundaries.

Lori, 34, was married for five years to a neglectful and emotionally abusive man. Lori left him and remarried. She is now in a relationship with a partner whom she can truly love and feel loved in return:

> I felt relieved when my marriage ended. After being with someone I wasn't in love with, it was a relief when it was finally over. I no longer had to argue with someone who made me feel bad about myself.

Shortly after my separation, I got lucky and met my current husband. I was going out with him for only three months when he proposed. At first I was somewhat hesitant to accept because I didn't know him very well. However, I felt he was being truly honest when he told me how much he loved me and wanted to take care of me and the kids. I made it clear to him that my kids would always come first, and I would never accept being treated like I had been by my ex.

Jay is completely different from my ex-husband. I can tell him how I feel about things without being afraid of being mistreated. He treats me very well. He supports and respects me. He walks around telling his friends that I'm his lady of leisure. He opened his wallet and his heart to me. We've been married three years, and I feel blessed to find someone so honest and loving. My second marriage made me a lot stronger and unafraid.

It is not uncommon for women to jump back into the dating scene soon after divorce. Their longing for companionship and intimacy, however, may lead them into a new relationship or marriage before they have mourned and healed from their previous one.

Despite the desire to find love, we should always remember that no matter how we feel about our former spouse, we once loved that person and need time to grieve the end of the relationship.

As part of the healing process, we need to learn how to trust again and work through feelings of anger, shame, and guilt that we may have experienced as a result of the break-up.

A second marriage may be a successful experience for some women. However, studies have shown that there is a high likehood of it failing.

But why is this so?

A great number of people who remarry fail to learn from their previous relationships. The most common reason is they tend to blame their former spouses for the outcome of their marriages and fail to acknowledge their own role and participation.

The problem is that, when we blame the failure of our marriage solely on our former spouse, we are likely to repeat with a new partner the same mistakes we made in our previous relationship.

It is difficult for many of us to look at ourselves and accept our shortcomings, or for that matter, to understand how our unresolved emotional issues could interfere with our ability to experience a satisfying relationship. Nevertheless, undertaking such an introspective will better prepare us to do things differently the next time around. In other words, it will allow us to understand what we need to work on, whether it be our fears and insecurities, unrealistic expectations, or lack of self-fulfillment.

Lori, for instance, seems to have entered a new relationship feeling more secure and less fearful of rejection and abandonment. Unlike her first marriage, she has been able to enforce her boundaries. Being able to assert her needs is helping Lori feel good about herself and experience a healthy relationship.

To find love, we need to first be on good terms with ourselves. If we experience strong feelings of inadequacy, difficulty with intimacy, or other unresolved emotional issues, we may find it difficult to trust, solve conflicts, or set boundaries in our intimate relationships. We are also more likely to attract emotionally unavailable partners. All of these things can greatly interfere with our ability to find love.

With that in mind, make it a priority to take care of yourself first before you look for romance. You do not want your fears and insecurities to get in the way of building a strong bond with the new person in your life. If you keep pursuing romantic relationships when you are not ready, you risk experiencing a great deal of disappointment in your search for love.

"I need you dad"

A Father's Role in a Woman's Life

While painful, experiencing a broken heart should not be thought of as a mostly sad chapter in our lives that we are eager to put behind us, but rather a reminder of what we have gained and learned.

So what can a woman possibly learn from discovering her partner's infidelity or experiencing the end of a marriage?

For Sarah, 37, who shared her story of being a victim of an extramarital affair, the disappointment and hurt in her love life compelled her to face her fears and insecurities. It also helped her reconnect with an important person in her life—her dad:

> This has been such an incredible journey for me from December to now. It's not been easy, though. Thinking of how scared I had been of leaving and how dependent I had been on Joe. But I did. I'm moving on with my life. I know I made the right decision; I couldn't handle anymore of what I was going through.

Every day the universe shows me something, and it's usually painful. But now I look at it in a positive way. All the little things that have happened along the way have helped me get to the point where I am now. Moving away from my husband was the right thing I needed to do for myself. I feel pretty good right now. If I had left a few months ago, I'd probably be back with him because I wasn't ready. I was so scared that I had to hide.

Now I'm looking forward to facing life head-on. For the first time I feel at peace, and I know what I'm doing is the right thing. Two or three weeks ago I didn't feel that way.

I've come so far with the help of my friends, family, and my therapist. I came to the realization that I can't control what Joe is doing or what he's done. I can only control what I'm doing. Knowing what I want and don't want for myself is important to me. I know there's no way in hell that I'm going to turn around and go back to the place where I was when I was married, or even where I was a month ago or two months ago. I know there's only one direction for me, and that's forward. That's where I'm going.

I feel so secure in myself. It doesn't matter what Joe thinks; I'm not going to get back together with him. If that's what he's thinking, he should forget it, there's no way! We were so unhappy when we were together, and he blames it all on me.

While this has been a difficult time in my life, something good happened. I contacted my dad, whom I hadn't seen in several years. I e-mailed him and said, "I need you. You're my dad, and I need to feel protected; I need to feel you're there for me." I never felt that way, which is probably why I ended up with Joe in the first place. I needed to feel protected and secure.

My dad called me, and it was wonderful. He told me how much he loved me. He helped my soul so much. I feel so secure and confident. It was the closure I had to have to reconnect with my dad. So that was a very good thing that happened to me. It was something I needed to do for a long time, and I wasn't willing to do it until a few weeks ago. I'm grateful for that.

For Sarah, the painful break-up of her marriage opened emotional wounds from her childhood. Once again, she had to deal with loss, abandonment, and rejection. During this most difficult time in her life, Sarah felt the need to turn to her dad and be re-assured of her lovability, which she may have missed growing up.

Being able to reconnect with her dad is allowing Sarah to begin healing from her past and coping with the negative feelings that resulted from the end of her marriage.

A dad is the first man in a woman's life, and our relationship with him affects our ability to develop healthy relationships with other men. From our relationship with our father, we learn what to expect in a man and how to relate to him.

What kind of relationship did I have with my dad while growing up? How close do I feel to him? Does he value, love and accept me? These are questions we should try to answer to have a better understanding of the relationship we have with our fathers.

The role of dads has changed over the years. For a majority of women, their dads were rarely involved in their daily lives, if at all. Nowadays, with an increasing number of women in the work force, dads are more actively participating in the upbringing of their children.

While many fathers are more involved in the lives of their daughters, they may not be aware of what their girls need from them and how the relationship should be like.

Dads may tend to perceive their role primarily as a provider and disciplinarian. They place their value as a dad mostly on their ability to succeed in these roles. When it comes to providing their daughters with the emotional security, love, and acceptance they need to develop into well adjusted women, they may feel their participation is not as important. They tend to underestimate the enormous amount of influence they have on the emotional well-being of their child.

Many fathers may find it easier to relate to their daughters when they are young. However, when their girl begins to mature sexually, some dads no longer know how to interact and show affection. As a result, they may distance themselves. When this happens, a girl is left dealing with the loss of a bond with her dad and all of the negative feelings that come with it.

A girl will find it difficult to relate to her dad if he is emotionally distant, overly critical or authoritarian. His behavior can make her feel insecure, rejected, and worthless.

No girl wants to experience feelings of anger and resentment toward her dad and thus rebel. Instead, she wants to be close to him and learn how to love, respect and value herself and others.

A girl wants her dad to show interest in her and accept who she is—her personality, the choices she makes, and her different views. If this fails to happen, she may have difficulty developing a strong bond with him. Being unable to have the relationship she desires and needs with her dad leaves a great void; an open wound that needs to be healed.

In a letter to her dad, Rachel, 36, opens her heart:

Dear Dad,

I remember those times when I was your little girl and you would put me on your lap and stroke my hair. I remember you kneeling down on the side of my bed to read me fairy tales. I remember lying down between you and mom on cold winter mornings and how safe I felt.

Dad, you tried so hard to make me happy by buying me everything I wanted. I know that seeing me cry would break your heart, and I must confess that I took advantage of that.

As I grew up and became a young lady, you treated me the same way you did when I was your little girl. You complimented me, showed affection, and never hurt me with mean or harsh words. I felt you loved and cared about me. I will always treasure that. I admired you so much, Dad, for being a smart, driven, and thoughtful man. People's misfortunes touched you so deeply, and I felt your compassion for them. Thanks for teaching me to be caring and loving and how to treat people with respect.

There are some things, however, that caused me pain and sadness. I tried so hard to gain your admiration, but I always felt I let you down. I don't remember, Dad, you ever saying "good job" or "I'm proud of you." I didn't feel like I met your expectations, whatever they were.

You never made me believe in my ability to succeed in anything. That's why I think I have tried so hard all my life to gain your admiration.

You were always so busy, Dad. I wished you were around more. I wish we had played and enjoyed each other more. There were so many places I wish you had taken me. If I could, I would have traded all the things you bought me for your time. I wish I was the number one thing in your life. I wish, Dad, that everything was perfect. That I had a perfect childhood, but it wasn't so.

The thing about my childhood that brings me the most sadness is when you would get home after drinking. I anxiously waited for you to get home every night. I remember how happy you made me when I would see your smiling face. Some nights, however, you came home drunk. You would look so serious, so distant. I felt so little, insignificant, and scared. Every night, I didn't know what to expect. When you would fight with mom, I was afraid, very afraid. I remember hearing you say that you were going to leave her and that made me so scared. I feared you would abandon me.

It took me a long time, Dad, to accept your weaknesses and let go of my resentment toward you for failing to meet all my expectations. I was able to let go when I became a mom. While I love my children the way you loved me, I still let them down at times. Like you, Dad, I learned that I also have my moments of insecurity.

The same way I expected you to accept and love me unconditionally, I also want to love you for the way you are. You did what you could, and I'm sure you never meant to hurt me. I will always hang on to the good memories of me and you, Dad. Those memories comfort my soul.

Your daughter,

Rachel

"We're best friends and lovers"

What a Successful Marriage Feels Like

Experiencing a fulfilling marriage does not mean marrying a flawless spouse or living a fairy tale. Couples who are content with their marriages did not necessarily wed their soul mates. Instead, they married a person who, like themselves, has both qualities and flaws. As in any marriage, they live through the highs and lows of a relationship, but unlike many others, they share a strong commitment to one another. They are aware of what it takes to keep their bond intact and put in the work to maintain it.

Louise, 37, Diana, 51, Annie, 48, and Tina, 28, share something in common: they all have successful marriages. They credit this to trust, respect, and effective communication.

Louise has been married for twelve years and is the mother of a ten-year-old girl:

> I like being married. To have a successful marriage, we can't idealize or expect our partner to be the way we want him to be. I believe that marriage fails

when there's a lack of communication, betrayal, or aggressiveness from either party. Marriage requires daily compromise and patience. It's only worth arguing about things that are important.

My marriage is working because my husband and I trust each other. Because of this, we give each other freedom. It's important that he respects my opinions and asks for my advice. When problems arise, we try to solve them right way. We both have our careers, and we're doing well. Before we married, we decided to get to know each other well, and that helped us a great deal.

This is what Diana has to say about her marriage of twenty-four years:

My husband and I are best friends and lovers. We don't agree on many things, but we're willing to hear each others points of view and reach a compromise. We respect each others feelings. I truly love my husband, and I believe he feels the same about me. He tells everybody how much he loves me.

Annie reflects on what makes her twenty-year marriage a success:

My husband listens to me; he understands me more than I understand myself. He's my cheerleader. He gives me advice and supports me. He accepts me the way I am. Marriage requires compromise, respect, and trust, and we have that in our marriage. My husband is a good man, and I always try to remember what I first liked about him—his generosity. I love him dearly.

Tina, a mother of two, is also content with her marriage:

> My relationship with my husband has been, for the most part, very good. We have a lot of respect for each other. My husband has many good qualities; he's compassionate, honest, sensitive, and affectionate. He spends time with me and the kids. He's not perfect, of course, but I don't allow his flaws to overshadow his qualities.

Julia, 52, shares similar values with her husband. He also supports and understands her. This has made her a happily married woman:

> I've been married for twenty-three years. My marriage seems to have everything it needs to succeed. My husband and I share the same values and have similar temperaments. We deal with our problems by talking about them and compromising. We give each other advice and respect one another. My husband is good at listening and supporting me in my decisions. He encourages and believes in me. I thank him for being the successful business woman I am today.

Laura, 26, doesn't find disagreement to be an obstacle in her marriage, but rather a way to strengthen the relationship:

> Despite being married for only a year, it's been a positive experience. My husband and I have different personalities, but this hasn't caused many arguments or conflicts between us. Instead, we've learned from

each other. I'm less impulsive since I got married, and I owe this to my husband.

In addition to effective communication, respect, and a satisfying sex life, 46-year-old Robin believes that being financially independent and content with herself has contributed to the success of her marriage:

> Marriage to me is an option in life that two people make. It can last forever or not. I got married at a later time in my life. I was financially independent and happy with my life. I believe this allowed me to face marriage with maturity and not with infantile illusions. I was able to see that two people with different personalities but the same goals can live well together when there's mutual respect, love, and tolerance.

> My husband and I make our relationship work by trying to communicate as soon as there's a problem. We try to solve the conflict so that whatever the problem is, it doesn't escalate. Another thing we do is not let sex come second, especially with the arrival of kids and the daily routine. I think couples tend to grow apart when sex no longer becomes important. Relationships also tend to fail when people marry with the expectation that their partners will solve all of their problems.

> In the first few years of my marriage, my husband and I were living apart because of our jobs. Being away from him made me realize he was the right person to share my happiness, frustrations, and accomplishments.

> If I had to go back in time, I wouldn't change anything about my marriage. I would have married the

same partner at the same time in my life and with the same simple ceremony. I look at my marriage as being eternal while it lasts. I believe that the most important thing is to live it day-by-day, whether it's a wonderful or difficult day.

Amy, 57, believes that her marriage has worked for so long because she found the complete package in her husband:

I've been married for thirty five years, and I love being married. I found in my husband everything I was looking for in a man: emotional and financial stability, companionship, and maturity. That's why I married someone much older then me; younger guys never interested me. My husband and I live in peace and harmony and, because of that, my marriage has been a great experience.

Teresa, 43, and Heather, 42, do not allow their partners' flaws to overcome their good qualities:

Teresa:

I'm somewhat frustrated with my marriage, more in relation to sex than anything else because it barely happens. However, I still believe that I have a good marriage compared to others that I know of. My husband is intelligent and hard working—God forbid I end up with a lazy man. We have similar interests. We both like to go to the ballet, opera, and movies. Jared isn't a womanizer and accepts my independence. I've heard other men saying they wouldn't accept that from their wives. What upsets me about him is that he gives up too easily on things. He also has mood swings, and this affects me a great deal. I came to the conclusion that he's the one who sets the tone of our relationship. If he's okay, I'm okay, because he doesn't bother me. I know he isn't everything I wanted in a man, but I don't feel like starting over with someone else because there will be other problems. I try to keep in mind the qualities that attracted me to him in the beginning and made me fall in love with him.

Heather:

My husband is an affectionate, honest, caring, and hard-working guy. He compliments me and is respectful. If I'm upset about something, he talks about the problem and makes an effort to compromise. His flaws are his lack of initiative and his inability to deal with his fears and insecurities. I wish he was more self-confident and willing to take chances in life. Even though some of his behaviors upset me at times, I don't let them overshadow the other qualities he has. I don't believe that I could ever meet a man better than my husband. There may be a guy who has other qualities that my husband doesn't, but he'll certainly have flaws that my husband doesn't have.

All of the previously mentioned marriages are working because there is mutual respect, trust, and commitment. Marital conflict is solved effectively, and verbal attacks or put downs are not tolerated. These women have the support of their husbands at an emotional level. The tremendous value they place on this is understandable. When we have a partner who is there for us, we feel important and loved.

Mutual acceptance is a critical component that helps strengthen a marriage. While these women are aware of their spouses' shortcomings, they refer to their men in a caring and loving way. That is, they are able to acknowledge their partners' good qualities and get the same in return.

Being able to value and admire our partner is critical to keeping us in love with him. We can esteem our husband for many reasons: for being intelligent, a good provider, an affectionate father, or a faithful husband. When a woman admires her spouse, he becomes valuable in her eyes. This in turn increases her respect and desire for him.

Laura, 37, has been married to a man she greatly admires:

> While I was dating my husband, we were young and at the time he didn't have a career. When we started discussing marriage, I decided to have a serious talk with him about family and his career plans. I'm a driven and determined person who also places great value on family. I wanted to marry someone who shared those same values. I find men who are lazy or who don't know what they're going to do with their lives extremely unattractive. I also don't appreciate men who put friends and work before family. Marrying a man with money wasn't a priority, but marrying someone without the desire to succeed was a big no for me. When my husband and I had a talk about his professional goals, he told me about his plan to go back to school and pursue a career in business. He also told me how much he'd like to be a dad. We've been married for twelve years, and I'm proud of my husband. I admire him immensely for being a hard

worker, a great father and good husband. There's no other man I'd rather be with.

Unlike Laura, there are a number of women who are no longer able to admire their spouses. As a result, the attraction fades, and the relationship turns into a source of discontent or even at times, deep regret. This actually occurs quite frequently, and it happened to Sharon, a 52-year-old business woman:

I was married for seven years, and it was the worst experience in my whole life. When I met my husband, we fell in love right away and, soon after, we decided to get married. We were poor, and getting married also helped with the expenses. A few years after we married, I decided to open a clothing store with a friend. It worked out well. We began making lots of money, and our business grew more than I ever expected.

As my business took off, I began traveling a lot. I had the chance to meet new people, and I became more confident and outgoing. I started taking care of my appearance and began attending social events. I was happy, wealthy, and professionally satisfied. The only thing that wasn't working was my marriage. I didn't have a husband, but a ghost. Unlike me, my ex-husband didn't accomplish anything. He kept his same job and was living off my money.

What irritated me the most about him was his lack of manners. He embarrassed me. I'd go to parties and events without him. I felt superior to him, and this didn't make me feel good. Eventually I fell out of love and there was nothing left to make me stay in the marriage. I filed for divorce. He resisted it at first, but ended up accepting.

We could not, however, reach an agreement, so we wound up in court. He left the marriage in pretty good financial shape. I had to give to him two of my apartments, some art pieces, my BMW, and a piece of land, among other things. I had to start from scratch, but it was worth it. I don't regret what I did because I'm free and happy. I'll never get married again. I have two boyfriends now, and I can say that my life is better than I hoped for.

While it is important that we see traits in our partner that we appreciate, we should not expect that he will share our same goals, values, and interests. We cannot turn our spouse into the person we want him to be. What we can do, however, is help bring out qualities in him that he already has. For instance, you are not going to make your husband be self-driven if that is not who he is. But if this is a trait he already possesses, you can help foster its growth.

Two people will never be alike, but their differences may not be significant if they are aware of how compatible they are with a potential partner. If people take this into account before they make the decision to take their intimate relationships to a higher level, they are increasing their chances of experiencing a successful marriage.

What often happens, however, is that when we are infatuated with someone who shares different views or values on important issues such as family, career, and religion, we may fail to foresee the impact this could have on a marriage. As time passes and the passion wears off, these differences may begin to interfere with our ability to admire, respect, and value our partner. Anger and resentment may build and become a major obstacle in the way of a healthy relationship.

Michelle, 32, is married to a man she doesn't admire:

> I've never been able to look up to my husband. We've been married fourteen years, and he's always been a person with no ambition. He doesn't have any desire to grow professionally and make a better life. This is a big turn off. I'd like him to be more determined and ambitious. We fight all the time because of this. I call him a loser. He doesn't say anything. His quietness also irritates me. I came to the conclusion that we have different personalities, that we have nothing in common.

Even though a couple may disagree on important issues, they can still build a strong relationship if they openly address their differences in a respectful, accepting, and compromising manner. By doing so, conflicts can be properly resolved, keeping their bond tight.

The strength of the bond between two people is what makes a marriage a rewarding and fulfilling journey. When a couple experiences a deep connection with one another, they feel loved, desired, and special. They share a sense of closeness and an ongoing feeling of romance.

All women look forward to romance in their marriages. The truth is that the most romance any of us will ever experience is during courtship and the newlywed phase of marriage. As the passion wears off and a couple is faced with an increasing number of responsibilities, such as raising a family and work, romance all too often begins to fade.

It is important, however, to have romance in our marriage to keep things lively. We have all heard of ways of creating romance, such as going out on dates, getaways, or surprising one another—the list is almost endless. While following such advice can be an exciting and entertaining way to break up the routine, it is not the main way romance should be experienced if the bond between two people is to be kept strong.

It is common for men to give their spouses flowers, jewelry, or other material things to make them happy, only to find themselves frustrated in the end. How long does a gift from your partner make you happy? Not long, I'm sure. Getting a beautiful ring will not make you settle for less in your relationship, right?

When we create romantic situations to bring passion back into our relationship or regain the feeling of closeness we once experienced with our partner, we may find ourselves feeling disappointed. While we may enjoy the gifts or surprises, it will not help strengthen a relationship that lacks intimacy. Vacations, dates, and other romantic events are highly enjoyable for couples who have a solid bond; it helps spice-up the relationship and keeps the marriage strong.

True romance, however, is not experienced by what money can buy; it is not about having dinner in a great restaurant or a big rock on your finger. Instead, it is about a kiss, a hug, a nice conversation, or a word of understanding and appreciation. It is about "You look pretty tonight," or "I appreciate what you do" and "I'm sorry." Words and actions make us feel special and desired and draw us close to our partner.

Romance, therefore, should happen during the routine of marriage and not only during special occasions. We need to feel loved, desired, and appreciated not only on date night, but every day, like after we come back home from work or after spending the day taking care of the kids.

Our partner also wants to feel desired and appreciated as much as we do. When he gets home from work he wants us to show that we are happy to see him. He wants us to be content with the relationship by being appreciative, loving and sexually responsive. This is what romance is all about for a man.

Unfortunately, true romance does not exist in a great number of marriages. This is because people stop showing their partners how important they are. They should instead try to win each others heart, as Lisa, 51, put it:

> If I could go back in time, I'd think long and hard before I got married. Being in love is not enough; it evaporates when the routine of marriage sinks in. People who are smart don't let this happen, though. They keep winning each others hearts, making their marriage last.

What we see happening quite often is not people trying to win their partners' hearts, but instead neglecting their needs. This is often the case when a couple becomes parents.

Many women would agree with the following comment from Laura, a 39-year-old college professor:

> I think any relationship changes over time, and a major reason is kids. We tend to give a lot of ourselves to our children and our husbands are no longer a priority. Unfortunately, when we try to recover the relationship, it's no longer possible.

Laura makes a valid point in how children take up a lot of our time. However, they should not be the reason why a marriage lacks romance or why we lose a connection with our partner.

We can all find time to be romantic and bond with our spouse because it does not take a whole lot of time to show love. Contrary to what some people may believe, we do not need to be creative to have romance in our intimate relationship.

When you look back at the courtship with your husband, you probably have great memories of the simple things you did together. Both of you were able to demonstrate how much you cared for each other, and this is what true romance is all about.

If you and your partner are able to develop a strong bond with each other, you are more likely to experience true romance in your relationship and be satisfied with your marriage. If, on the other hand, you are frustrated in your attempts to connect with your spouse, you may experience loneliness, sadness, and resentment. No romantic dinner or gift will make things better. Both of you will continue to grow apart from each other and may mistakenly blame work or children for the lack of romance.

If you believe your marriage lacks true romance, take an honest look at the relationship. Assess what is missing and what you and your partner can do to strengthen your marital bond. Of critical importance is to reflect on how both of you show love for one another. This is the fundamental core of a long and prosperous marriage.

We owe it to ourselves to experience joy and fulfillment in our intimate relationships. None of us deserve to spend a great part of our lives feeling cheated and unhappy because we married someone who falls short of the person we envisioned ourselves with. Our marriage should not be seen as the worst experience of our lives, but rather something we feel blessed to have.

 # "I'd like more affection"

Sexual Intimacy and Marriage

A critical component that is missing in many marriages is a gratifying sex life. Sexual intimacy helps a couple grow closer, strengthening the bond they share.

A number of married couples experience a satisfying sex life. This is the case of April, 40, married for eight years and the mother of a five-year-old boy:

> Before I got married, Vance and I already enjoyed sex quite a lot. After we had our son, our sex life began to change because we had little time for ourselves. However, we talked about it and decided that sex should be as important as our careers, our child, and our life at home. In the same way that it's important for a couple to share similar values and beliefs, they should also consider sex before judging whether or not their marriage will work. The sexual aspect of an intimate relationship is as important as mutual respect and acceptance. My husband and I nurture those aspects of our marriage.

Having sex is not the same as making love, and this difference is clear to women. The former involves sexual release and pleasure with little or no emotional involvement. The latter, on the other hand, is not just sex; it is an act of emotional connection with the person we love. When we make love, we are cuddling, caressing, and exchanging affection. And this is what we want out of our sex life. This is what Cindy, 55, longs for in her marriage:

> My husband and I used to make love all the time; however, over the years the intensity decreased. Because of our schedules, we barely see each other. We don't have a chance to have sex often, maybe once a month. I miss him. I miss the physical contact; it makes me feel happy and closer to him. In regard to quality, I believe he doesn't quite meet my expectations anymore. I'd like more affection, kisses, and hugs. I'd like to be complemented and, above all else, desired. All of these things we should receive without asking.

The sexual component of a marriage is critical for the relationship to succeed; therefore, it needs to be addressed when it becomes a source of dissatisfaction.

If you feel that your sex life is missing intensity, passion, or emotional connection, you need to discuss this with your partner. Share your feelings and expectations with him. When a couple is committed to the relationship, both partners are willing to meet one another half way.

The frequency of sexual activity in a great number of marriages is less than one or both partners desire. While sexual drive declines naturally after a certain age, physical and psychological factors can interfere with one's desire to be sexual. Low testosterone, lifestyle, and medications are common causes for a decrease or loss of sexual desire. Psychological factors such as stress, depression, and dissatisfaction with the relationship can also reduce one's libido.

Infrequent love making is a source of conflict in a number of marriages, including Donna's, a 41-year-old dental assistant. Here she explains what she expects from her husband to help make her love life more intense and pleasurable:

> My sex life? Oh, God, it was all the time, it was great. However, it began to change when we had our son. I was tired, and I had other priorities, and my husband didn't get the hang of it. I had to put my child to bed, feed him, change his diaper, and all the other things. I had no time left to be intimate with my husband.
>
> As my child got older, my husband and I started having sex more often. However, it all changed again when I went off the pill because of my blood pressure. When that happened, I began to feel uncomfortable having sex; I didn't want to risk getting pregnant again.
>
> I took responsibility for everything until I wanted to have a baby. I even thought about getting my tubes tied, but other women told me not to because it's a major surgery. I've told my husband that the rubber thing is no fun. It's like, "Wait a second." It's not spontaneous; it's not fun for me.
>
> I resent that my husband hasn't taken care of it. I told him to go do something about it, but he hasn't. We could have so much fun doing what we used to do. At the same time, as a woman, I feel guilty for not having sex as much as my husband wants. I know

he resents the fact that our sex life is not as intense. However, right now having sex is not fun for me. It's like, "Are you done yet?"

I'd like my husband to be nice and seduce me. I'd give him twelve blow jobs all night long if he would just be nice instead of coming home bitching about how fucked up his day was and how hard he worked or how much he does. Blah, blah, blah. "Oh, that makes me hot, baby!" Why doesn't he come to me and say, "Hi, how was your day, honey?"

Men and women view sex and intimacy differently. While we primarily seek companionship, respect, and affection from our spouse to feel close to him, he on the other hand uses sexual activity to express his love and to connect with us. When we respond positively to our partner's sexual advances, he feels reassured of his masculinity and desirability, and this in turn helps boost his self-esteem.

If, instead, we turn him down sexually on a frequent basis, his entire being may feel rejected. This can trigger feelings of resentment, which he may express through passive aggressive or hostile behavior. A common reaction is for him to distance himself, both physically and emotionally.

Unlike men, who primarily use sex to bond with their partners, we need to experience an emotional connection outside the bedroom before we desire to be sexually intimate.

If our partner behaves in a disrespectful, rejecting, or neglectful manner, we do not look forward to being intimate. While we may still desire sexual intercourse, we may not desire to be sexual with him. If we do so, it may not feel right. Here is what Kim, 38, and Laura, 42, have to say:

Kim:

> My first husband didn't understand why I didn't want to have sex after we fought. He wasn't being my friend, and it didn't feel right. It doesn't matter how well he did it. I felt grossed out. I felt used. I definitely felt that way. Even with my husband right now, if I'm upset with him, I can't have sex for a few days. For him, however, sex is a way to make up. "Oh, we get to make up now." He doesn't understand the problem we just had.

Laura:

> My ex wanted to have sex even though he hated me. I had sex whenever he wanted to because I was trying to be good. I was trying to work toward fixing my marriage. I was trying to be nice, but he hated me, and that was an amazing conflict for me to be in. It was a horrible thing, having sex with someone who hates you. That was sexual abuse. I think that's a problem when we try too hard to fix things.

Love making is a beautiful act between two people who share deep feelings for one another. Therefore, it should never be used to humiliate, gain control, or expose the other person's flaws. When this happens, a person is likely to experience shame and guilt. These feelings can make a couple grow apart, causing irreparable damage to their bond. Carrie's relationship may be heading down this road. Here is what this 22-year-old has to say:

I'm my boyfriend's first, but he's not mine, and he's mad because of this. He blames me for not saving myself for him, and he uses this against me. He can't get over it. He tells me that he thinks about this every day. He forces me to think about it. He makes me feel junky. He says that he saved himself and that I didn't. I told him I'm sorry, but that I can't do anything about it. In the beginning of our relationship, he accepted that I wasn't a virgin, but now that he fell in love with me, it's been hard for him. What bothers me most is when he tells me that he doesn't think he's special. He's become obsessed with it and wants us to go to counseling.

There is nothing more important for us than to feel unconditionally loved. We are likely to feel insecure, rejected, and guilty when our spouse expresses his dissatisfaction with the way we behave, our appearance, or our ability to meet his sexual needs.

A common thought is, am I failing as a wife? Is he going to turn to another woman? Is he going to leave me? Our fears and insecurities may become a threat to our emotional well-being and ultimately our marriage.

Ellen, 52, shares about her husband's expectations of their sex life and how it affects her:

I've been married for twenty-three years, and everything was going well until our sex life began to interfere with our marriage. In the beginning of our marriage and until a few years ago, everything was going good with our sex life. My husband used to accept me the way I was, a woman who's a little shy and reserved in relation to sex. We never had a creative sex life, and I never felt he was expecting more from me. He was also reserved when making love to me.

However, about two years ago everything started changing. I began to notice a change in our sex life, or better yet, when my husband makes love to me. He's less gentle and more aggressive. He expects more from me. He wants more creativity and eroticism, and I'm failing to meet his sexual fantasies. I don't feel comfortable doing certain things he'd like me to do in bed.

We've talked about this several times, but he tries to convince me that we should explore our sex lives to experience more pleasure. It's been difficult for me because I like sex that's calm, with lots of touching and caressing. I don't need to add fantasy to our sex life to increase pleasure.

Not being able to meet my husband's expectations is making me feel anxious and depressed. I feel insecure and afraid that this could ruin my marriage. This has been the only thing that's changed in my relationship during my twenty-three years of marriage.

As we grow older, we tend to be self-conscious about the way we look. This can affect our perception of how desirable we feel to our partner.

If our spouse complements us and shows his attraction, he is reassuring us of our desirability. This, in turn, makes us more comfortable to expose our bodies and express ourselves sexually.

On the other hand, if our spouse makes negative comments about our looks, we feel insecure, ashamed, and rejected. Since it is difficult to bond with someone who is rejecting, we may find ourselves unable to enjoy lovemaking. This is also true when our spouse is emotionally distant, neglectful, or abusive.

All of us desire a wholesome union with our partner, which includes a satisfying sex life. A healthy sexual relationship, however, is only possible when we develop an emotional bond with our partner. This is because when we make love, we are unveiling not only our bodies, but our inner selves. It is far from just a release of sexual energy, but an act of surrender. When we surrender ourselves to someone we care about, we want to trust that we will be respected and loved. This makes our sexual encounters not only physically gratifying, but emotionally rewarding as well.

"I've always feared getting married"

The Single Woman

Not all women choose to marry. Some opt for a relationship without the formal commitment of marriage while others have romantic involvements without taking their relationship to the next level.

Jamie, a 59-year-old accountant, and Carla, a 54-year-old business woman, were never married and have no plans to ever tie the knot:

Jamie:

> I never got married, and I never will. I had a few serious relationships that lasted about four or five years. I felt in love, but it was hard to see myself getting married. I never miss being married because I've always liked my independence. It was my decision to be single. I've always wanted to live life to the fullest and, by getting married, I'd have to give up a lot.

Carla:

> Getting married; how? I'm controlling, dominant, and a perfectionist. I have high expectations of others, and I like to tell people what to do. I hate people who doubt my abilities and intelligence. Marriage is not for me. I'm perfectly fine being in a relationship without committing to marriage.

Unlike Jamie and Carla, Clair, 64, wanted to get married, but never met the ideal man:

> For most of my adult life I got involved in brief romantic relationships. I met a lot of nice guys over the years, but always believed I could find someone better. I was constantly trying to find the ideal match. I wanted to get married, but only to the right person. Unfortunately, it never happened.

Like Claire, there are women who have a strong desire to marry, but complain of not being fortunate enough to find a soul mate. These women get involved in romantic relationships, but before long they pick their partners to pieces until the attraction they once felt is lost. They move from relationship to relationship in search of the idealized partner, truly believing he can be found. Since everyone has faults, no one will ever be good enough in these women's eyes, and the search for a soul mate is destined to end in disappointment.

People who are "too picky" may be holding onto unrealistic expectations of a partner. They may do so because of their difficulty accepting people's flaws, which could be related to their inability to accept their own shortcomings.

A person's tendency to idealize a mate may also be related to fear of commitment. This fear can cause someone to go back and forth with the same partner, or get into relationships where there's little chance of experiencing true love.

But what causes this fear of commitment?

With commitment comes the quest for intimacy, and for some people this can be quite threatening. When we become emotionally close to someone we love, we experience a sense of dependency which can be frightening, especially if we have strong feelings of inadequacy and low self-esteem.

When we see ourselves in a positive light, we look forward to form and maintain a tight bond with a partner. However, if we view ourselves as being flawed, inferior, and unlovable, we may anticipate getting hurt through rejection, betrayal, and abandonment. This, as a result, can move us further away from commitment.

Lori's feelings of inadequacy contribute to her fear of rejection and abandonment in her intimate relationship. Here is what this 24-year-old college student has to say:

> I'm insecure. Sometimes my boyfriend does things that I know are not a big deal, but my way of thinking makes me believe he doesn't care about me as much as I care about him. My fears are getting in the way of me having a good relationship with him. When I feel insecure, I feel more dependent and cling to him even more. By doing so, I push him away. I don't see myself ever getting married.

Some people may avoid being in a committed relationship for fear of being controlled and losing their own identities. Such individuals may have difficulty setting boundaries or resolving conflicts. By avoiding commitment, they are trying to protect themselves from what they believe is inevitable—disappointment and hurt.

People who have difficulty emotionally committing to a partner may not have been exposed to healthy role models early in life. How our parents interacted with one another has a strong influence on how we behave toward our partner as well as our expectations of what an intimate relationship should be like.

Some of us grew up in families where there was little or no healthy intimacy. Our parents were emotionally distant from each other and often communicated using critical, judgmental, and condescending talk. Their relationship with us was not warm and comforting enough to make us feel secure and accepted. As a result, we were deprived of learning about unconditional love, trust, and respect, which is what healthy intimacy is all about. Instead, we learned to fear emotional closeness.

As we become adults, we carry the residue of our childhood experiences, and they may manifest themselves into our fear of developing a bond with a romantic partner. While a part of us desires building a deep connection with someone we love, the other part fears rejection, abandonment, and failure. If these fears are increasingly amplified, we hurt our chances of experiencing a satisfying intimate relationship.

Erica, 51, seems to be experiencing this conflict:

It was my option not to get married. I've always feared getting married. I had many boyfriends, but when they wanted to get serious, I would leave them. As I got older, I became more selective. My parents are divorced, and I witnessed a lot of things that still bother me. I'm afraid of getting married and not being happy like my mother. I've decided not to risk it. At times I miss having a companion, someone who likes me, listens to me, and supports me. Someone I can share my life with. However, the past always comes to mind, and I remember that men are all the same, selfish womanizers who are, for the most part, immature. Therefore, I try to be happy on my own. I try not to feel lonely, but the future scares me.

If you are a person who has reservations about committing to an intimate relationship, you need to first acknowledge your fears, then work on them. Looking into your past can be helpful in identifying the origins of your fears and insecurities and how they have affected the decisions concerning your love life. Revisiting your past will also give you the opportunity to reflect on what degree the difficulties with your romantic relationships resemble those of your parents and what changes you need to make to fulfill your need for love and connection.

For many years Pamela, a 44-year-old school teacher, was unable to move forward with her intimate relationships. She was able to commit to a partner and contemplate marriage only when she came to understand how her upbringing, especially the relationship with her dad, was interfering with her ability to experience true love:

I haven't gotten married because for a long time I didn't feel confident about the men I dated. Today I feel secure about myself and my partner's feelings for me. I've been able to understand how my family, especially my dad, has affected my relationships. My dad is an authoritarian and controlling person. He never approved any of my boyfriends and didn't support me in any way. We never got along well. When I would bring a boyfriend home, he would make negative comments about him. Over the years I had a chance to meet a few wonderful men, but the relationship would never last long. I had frequent angry outbursts and wasn't willing to put up with their flaws.

When I reached my forties, I realized I was a single, middle-age woman living at home with my parents. That didn't make me feel good. I then began to reflect on myself and my relationship with men. I came to the conclusion that my dad's behavior toward me and his desire to keep me under his control was stopping me from being happy.

Once I realized that, I decided to make changes. When I met my current boyfriend, I was able to stand firm and not let my father, once again, ruin my relationship. I gained courage and moved out of my parents' house. My dad, of course, disapproved; he still barely talks to me, but I'm okay because I know I did the right thing.

My boyfriend and I have been together for four years. I've learned to control my temper and accept him the way he is. We have a great relationship. We share the same interests; we both like to travel, cook, and spend time with each other. There's no aggressiveness, demands, or jealousy between us.

This is the first time in my life that I see myself getting married.

Our fears underlie many of our difficulties in life. We all want to make the right decisions and feel at peace with ourselves. However, this is not possible when we allow our fears to take control of us. We know this is the case when we feel overwhelmed by sadness, worry, anxiety, and self-doubt.

Our negative thoughts and feelings can deprive us of power, self-confidence and hope. We need to overcome them with positive thoughts and actions. Fear should never be stronger than our determination to make our brief existence on this earth meaningful and fulfilling.

Women's Words
of Advice

All of us hear words of advice from the different people in our lives. Most things are said with the intent of helping us make the right decisions. While we reflect upon and follow some of the advice, much of it becomes just words that we soon forget.

When it comes to love, we all tend to be less receptive to suggestions, especially when they threaten our self-esteem or when they go against what we would like to believe. We do not want, for instance, to hear someone telling us that the person we are madly in love with does not share the same feelings for us. This can cause us deep pain and sadness. Likewise, we may not want to hear that a marriage will present us with many more challenges and difficulties than we ever anticipated. Instead, we want to believe that being in love will inevitably lead to a happily-ever-after marriage.

When we are infatuated, any advice that does not serve to intensify our positive feelings for our partner is not fully processed by our brain. This advice is disregarded because it does not match the fairy tale story we want to live. When we enter a marriage, we want to believe that it will turn out the way we expect.

Time, however, shows us that while sharing a life with someone we love can bring personal fulfillment, it will never match all of our expectations. Some of them were unrealistic to begin with.

When the day comes that we are faced with unexpected disappointment, we may find ourselves reflecting upon words that were once said to us, especially by other women who have gone through similar life experiences. We may no longer think of the advice as just words from women we once thought of as bitter, or who had the misfortune of experiencing an unhappy marriage. We will think of them instead as a confirmation that all women share similar dreams and expectations and, through experience, learn the truth about love and marriage.

The following women share their advice on intimate relationships and marriage. Here's what they have to say:

Brenda, 38, and Katie, 33, advice is to watch for warning signs:

"One day I was driving into town and my husband, who was my boyfriend at the time, called to ask if I was marrying him just for his money," Brenda stated.

"What did that show you?" I asked.

"That he had trust issues. But I thought, no problem. I know he trusts me and everything is going to be fine. But it wasn't. I should have taken that as a sign of how things were going to be. He turned out to be a controlling and selfish person who never loved or cared about me."

For Katie, small lies are a major sign to watch for: "As soon he says one little lie, it's okay to turn and run because that's not one little lie, but a future of bigger and bigger lies."

Brenda, a 38-year-old divorcee, advises to not stay in a relationship too long if it is not working:

> Follow your instincts. With the first punch, get rolling. Move away from the negative situation, don't wait too long. I did. I waited too long. We tend to blame ourselves when things don't go well. We always hope that things are going to get better, but if they don't, you shouldn't be afraid to leave. Don't be afraid that he won't want you back. If you separate yourself from that, the ball will start rolling to one direction. Either it's going to fail or it's going to move forward; you always have those choices. Hopefully it'll go forward in a positive direction. If the marriage fails, you go forward, you pursue your future. You get to be strong, you get to have some balls.

Signing a prenuptial agreement and leaving a relationship that has the potential of being abusive is the advice of Carla, a 37-year-old mother of two boys:

> Get out! When you see the signs of emotional abuse, you've just got to go. It's not going to change. You certainly can't change him. We see a lot of women in unhappy relationships not being able to leave. They lack power. Guys tend to have more power, financial power. A lot of women don't have their own money. I didn't have my own money when I was married. You have to keep your own money, you have to save. If a woman isn't financially

independent, if there's no partnership, if the guy has a huge income and she's at home with the kids, there should be a way to secure herself, her own bank account or something.

When I got married, my ex-husband told me that I shouldn't worry, but I found out a year later he had a joint account with his mother and the reason was so that I couldn't touch it. I ended up with nothing. If I could advise someone I would say go and see an attorney and have some kind of agreement. Get an attorney before you get married and have the attorney make some kind of prenuptial agreement that's going to protect you both, particularly you.

Like Carla, Lucy, 41, suggests signing a prenuptial and getting to know a partner and his family very well:

My advice is to meet the family. See what you're up against and live with your partner for at least two years. Get to know him and his habits. Sign a prenuptial. I regret not doing it. I wasn't offered it. If there's money involved, I'd get a lawyer. Some people don't want to do it because it sounds unromantic, but you never know. It makes it easier down the road.

Joy, 37, also recommends that women get to know their partner's parents well and talk with ex-girlfriends if at all possible:

You should always talk with the ex-girlfriends. They're an important source of information. Definitely meet the parents and the entire family. Spend a lot of time with them. The parents will usually seem nice when you first meet them, but you have to spend a lot of time to get to know them well. They can cause major problems in your marriage down the road.

Claudia, 38, advises women to pay close attention to a partner's relationship with his mother. She also finds it important for a woman to pursue her own goals:

> A woman should try to know her future husband's family extremely well, especially the relationship with his mother. The way he treats his mom will shadow the way he'll treat his wife. He should not, however, be too close to his mother as this can be unhealthy. I also advise women to have a college degree or know what they want to do with their lives before they get married. They need to feel passionate about something other than getting married.

Tanya, 55, and Terry, 51, encourage women to know who they are and be happy with themselves before they commit to a marriage:

Tanya:

> I believe that if a woman doesn't take responsibility for her marriage, it'll ultimately fail. Also, if she gets married thinking it'll solve her problems, she's setting herself up for disappointment. Before deciding to marry, all women should get to know themselves well. My advice is to get married when you're mature enough, financially independent, and have your own personal issues resolved. Don't get married if you're unhappy with yourself. Also, don't depend on your partner financially. This will give him too much power over you.

Terry:

Advice? Don't get married thinking that it's the secret to your happiness, because you'll be disappointed. If you still don't know who you are and have no goals for yourself other than getting married, don't do it. Your marriage will be like a Band-aid on a gaping wound. It'll just serve to cover your unhappiness. When the fairy tale ends, you'll have to face what you've been avoiding all along.

Jenny, 47, believes women should be prepared for disappointment in their marriages:

My advice is to be prepared; your husband won't change for you. Also, don't expect that he's going to be your best friend or someone who will listen to you. Only gay friends do that. They're also the only ones who give honest compliments.

Melissa, 64, suggests that single women think carefully before deciding to marry:

Getting married is like succeeding in a career. You need to have the right skills. Not every woman was born to get married. The daily routine of a marriage is stressful. You need to know how to deal with new situations and not let your fantasies about your ideal man take over reality.

If I had to give advice to younger and unmarried people, I'd tell them to think long and hard before they get married. A couple needs to be mature enough to handle the daily challenges of a marriage and the raising of a family. Both people need to be in harmony with themselves and not seek marriage as a solution for loneliness.

Kimberly, 40, has the following advice:

If you don't feel like getting married, don't do it, even if you do have a child. Do it on your own. You don't need a man to support you—you can do it yourself. If you don't have a child and he already lied to you, don't go out with him. Likewise, if you have any kind of negative feeling toward him, just break it off. He'll end up hurting you bad down the road. Remember to be picky. Really picky.

"Do you think women aren't picky?" I asked.

"I think they're afraid of being alone," Kimberly replied.

All of us have our own romantic experiences that help shape our view of love and intimate relationships. Some we treasure, while others we try to forget. Regardless of how they turned out, we should remember that at one point, these relationships brought us happiness.

As human beings, we have been given the gift of love. However, love alone is not enough in our pursuit of a wholesome relationship. We also need to take responsibility by reflecting on our own choices, acting with appropriate caution, and having a firm grasp on reality. When we make decisions concerning our romantic lives, a coming together of the heart and mind will give us the best chance to experience love at its fullest.

Final Thoughts

We all have our own love stories to remember. In the blink of an eye we can relive our first kiss, a passionate night of love making, or a promise of eternal love; so many incredible moments that turn into unforgettable memories.

While love can give us a taste of magic, it also presents us with a touch of reality. All of us have experienced times of hurt, sadness, and disappointment in our intimate relationships. Which of us hasn't cried over a lost love, been hurt at the sound of a harsh word, or experienced the pain of not being hugged when we needed it most?

In our search for love we may stumble and fall along the way. When down, we may question what went wrong, shed tears, and struggle to console ourselves. We may feel lonely, confused, and unsure of what direction to take. But no matter how broken we are, nothing should keep us down. We have in our core the strength to pull ourselves up because we are, after all, women.

About the Author

Daniela Granzotto, Psy.D. is a licensed psychologist and psychotherapist. In her clinical practice she specializes in the treatment of depression, anxiety disorders, and relationship issues. Dr. Granzotto lives in Honolulu, Hawaii with her husband and two children.

BUY A SHARE OF THE FUTURE IN YOUR COMMUNITY

These certificates make great holiday, graduation and birthday gifts that can be personalized with the recipient's name. The cost of one S.H.A.R.E. or one square foot is $54.17. The personalized certificate is suitable for framing and will state the number of shares purchased and the amount of each share, as well as the recipient's name. The home that you participate in "building" will last for many years and will continue to grow in value.

HABITAT FOR HUMANITY

THIS CERTIFIES THAT

__YOUR NAME HERE__

HAS INVESTED IN A HOME FOR A DESERVING FAMILY

1985-2010

TWENTY-FIVE YEARS OF BUILDING FUTURES
IN OUR COMMUNITY ONE HOME AT A TIME

1200 SQUARE FOOT HOUSE @ $65,000 = $54.17 PER SQUARE FOOT
This certificate represents a tax deductible donation. It has no cash value.

Here is a sample SHARE certificate:

YES, I WOULD LIKE TO HELP!

I support the work that Habitat for Humanity does and I want to be part of the excitement! As a donor, I will receive periodic updates on your construction activities but, more importantly, I know my gift will help a family in our community realize the dream of homeownership. ***I would like to SHARE in your efforts against substandard housing in my community!*** *(Please print below)*

PLEASE SEND ME _____ SHARES at $54.17 EACH = $ $_____

In Honor Of: _____

Occasion: (Circle One)   HOLIDAY   BIRTHDAY   ANNIVERSARY

    OTHER: _____

Address of Recipient: _____

Gift From: _____ *Donor Address:* _____

Donor Email: _____

I AM ENCLOSING A CHECK FOR $ $_____ PAYABLE TO HABITAT FOR HUMANITY <u>OR</u> PLEASE CHARGE MY VISA OR MASTERCARD *(CIRCLE ONE)*

Card Number _____ Expiration Date: _____

Name as it appears on Credit Card _____ Charge Amount $ _____

Signature _____

Billing Address _____

Telephone # Day _____ Eve _____

PLEASE NOTE: Your contribution is tax-deductible to the fullest extent allowed by law.
Habitat for Humanity • P.O. Box 1443 • Newport News, VA 23601 • 757-596-5553
www.HelpHabitatforHumanity.org